Robert H. Brown

History of the Barrage at the Head of the Delta of Egypt

Vol. 2

Robert H. Brown

History of the Barrage at the Head of the Delta of Egypt
Vol. 2

ISBN/EAN: 9783337227333

Printed in Europe, USA, Canada, Australia, Japan

Cover: Foto ©ninafisch / pixelio.de

More available books at **www.hansebooks.com**

ARDEN

A NOVEL

BY

A. MARY F. ROBINSON

IN TWO VOLUMES
VOL II.

LONDON
LONGMANS, GREEN, AND CO.
1883

All rights reserved

CONTENTS

OF

THE SECOND VOLUME.

CHAPTER		PAGE
XIII.	Eyes and no Eyes	1
XIV.	In the Hill of Venus	23
XV.	A Good Resolution	38
XVI.	Lost and Found	52
XVII.	Friends	67
XVIII.	The Little Rift	76
XIX.	Pigskin will Last	90
XX.	I'll Love you True	109
XXI.	Woo'd, Married, and a'	119
XXII.	Needles and Pins	137
XXIII.	Old Friends	149
XXIV.	Two's Company	161

CONTENTS OF THE SECOND VOLUME.

CHAPTER		PAGE
XXV.	Stratford-on-Avon	181
XXVI.	Laughing and Crying	199
XXVII.	The Witnesses	208
XXVIII.	Afterwards	224
	Epilogue	238

ARDEN.

CHAPTER XIII.

EYES AND NO EYES.

ARDEN began her picture, and talked and thought of little else by day, and dreamed of it by night. It was not, you see, merely a work of art; it was a future, or rather the possible resurrection of her past. The canvas, representing a brilliant appleyard full of crimson and yellow fruit, floored with vivid aftermath, shot and streaked with sunlight, was be sent to Birmingham Exhibition, was, of course, to be accepted, to be sold for fifty pounds, and to fetch in many even higher-priced commissions.

Then she would go back to Rome; Arden sometimes thought, and always dreamed, that she would find her father there, and indeed without him she could not even imagine Rome. His sudden loss had had a strange effect upon her, one only possible in a person tenacious in affection, dense of perception, subject to an unimaginative, practical, but all-pervading dreaminess. Since she came to England she had never felt the keen despair that most girls would have felt in her situation; life did not seem in the least over for her; on the other hand, she was roused to an impatience, an activity quite foreign to her disposition, by an odd, unformulated conviction that her father, her happiness, her home, were being hidden from her; were, not lost, but secreted in some unknown place which it was not hopeless to discover. She had the superstitious clinging to the lost, which makes religious people spend half their lives in a Paradise, where all that has been taken from them remains unchanged by death. Arden, who could not realise a future different to the past, who yearned so passionately for the present, fancied Paradise an invention of the early Tuscan painters for the sake of charmingly contrasted pictorial effects; yet she had something of the same idea, but applied it differently. With her, too, the bitterness of death was robbed of its sting, the cruel realisation of hopeless, irremediable, eternal loss. Arden, too, had her Paradise.

Was it so very strange? Are many beliefs, for which martyrs have died, which in their turn have sacrificed an army of martyrs, are the great beliefs of the world so much better founded, so much more capable of being reasoned, so much firmer on a clearly-posed logical basis, than this superstition, born of dim anxious yearning, of refusal to accept the worst, this immortalisation of memory in the mind of a young and dreamy woman?

Meanwhile, the working at her picture brought her into constant contact with the people at the Farm. Gradually she became aware that, apart from the satisfaction of painting, there was a certain pleasure in going to the Williams's. They were always so glad to see her. There was no doubt that after the constrained, burdened, silent life of the Bushes it was pleasant to listen to Susie's eager determined theories as she sat by Arden's side in the sun-shot orchard, her chin propped in her palm, appealing, indignant, throwing her whole heart into every question, moral, social, artistic; always turning her words into opinions, her opinions into theories, her theories into combats, and in the strength and militance of her decision, ignoring the semi-accidental cause of it.

Perhaps, after all, the great charm was that this resolute, convinced young theorist paid Arden every homage that respect, affection, sympathy could suggest. Arden had seen so much, could talk about Rome, Pompeii, Syracuse, Florence, as Harry talked of Raynham and Faversham; she could answer so many questions, solve so many doubts, confirm so many suppositions. Moreover, she was beautiful, delicate, refined, an orphan. To Susie's ardent and chivalrous temperament each of these qualities was alone a reason for devoted attachment. Arden, therefore, always found herself treated as the supreme court of appeal by a pleader of character and intellect far stronger than her own. Lonely, weak, neglected, she was not insensible to the flattery. The brother also interested her, though she saw but little of him. Probably, had she known him better, she would have cared less. As it was, the constant half-allusions, unsaid praises, profound admiration of Harry in Susie's conversation, was not without effect. She remembered that on her first interview with him he had impressed her as a person of much kindness and energy. She was glad little Susie had so excellent a brother, and when she looked at the swampy or arid fields and the unkempt drive of the Bushes she contrasted them, in her own mind, with Harry Williams's management of his affairs.

So without any active interest, always with the feeling that this acquaintance was merely a stop-gap, she grew accustomed to find the Williams's a familiar part of her surrounding world. While she was painting her picture and dreaming of the future she gave a facile, half-attention to Susie's eager kindness, to her mother's well-meant fussinesses; and though she set them down as nothing, they sank deeper than she knew; for, at this time, the only three people in the world who seemed to care much if she coughed or sang, if she sighed or laughed, waked or slept, all lived at Woodleigh Farm.

It was strange, perhaps, that after such a different society Arden should be satisfied with simple farmers. But she never dreamed of seeking their society. She went to the Farm to paint, never for any other reason; she herself was unaware how much real friendliness the kindness and interest of these rustic people had awakened for them in her heart. At present she still ostensibly regarded them as the proprietors of the orchard.

One day Mrs. Lawrance, seeing Arden take up her hat and leave the parlour, followed her to the hall door.

'So you're aäf again to Williams's?'

'Yes; to my picture.'

'You're allus arter that girl, now.'

'Oh no, Mrs. Lawrance; I don't see her even, sometimes. I'm only painting the orchard.'

'And when will you a-done with it—th' archard?'

'It depends a good deal on the weather. If this sort of weather goes on, not till the end of the month.'

'Ay, ay; you're allus puling and pining, Sylvie; fretting or frabbing at summut. If you was less ignorant you'ld ha' perceived the turnips was at last extremities for want of rain.'

'Very likely. Italian turnips are more to my taste; they get their rain and their disagreeableness all in a lump.'

'Ah! 'Tis a pity you ever left your Italians!'

'Indeed, yes. But let me sell my picture, and then to damp skies and England, *Buonanotte*!'

Arden ran down the drive, letting fly the last sentence. She was sufficiently cross to feel a certain satisfaction in imagining how ungrateful and unkind her last words would seem to Mrs.

Lawrance. But nothing was too hard for such a cross-grained old woman. Her grandfather she really liked and cared for —but Mrs. Lawrance! Arden's dislike was perhaps sharpened by the suspicion that Mrs. Lawrance possessed more strength of feeling and capacity for fine action than all the true Lawrances together. Superior qualities are exasperating in a person one detests. By this time the girl was at the drive-gate. Her passion was cooled, and she felt a little repentant, but the sense of being in the way made her still more anxious to get away from this England of lush boggy greenness, of spongy outlines, thick air, untremulous and dull, skies without atmosphere, summers without glory or prostration, where she was always cross, fatigued, and in the wrong. Oh, she did not see the moment of getting away!

As she mused thus, leaning her arms on the high gate and her head on her arms, she looked idly down the lane towards the bridge.

'Miss Lawrance,' cried a fresh provincial voice from the side. It was Susie, walking briskly, a little basket on her arm.

'I've been to the Boltons',' she explained, 'for we ran out of yeast. I thought I should find you at home—aren't you going to paint to-day, Miss Lawrance?'

'Paint! Oh yes—everything depends on that!'

'May I walk with you down the lane?'

'I shall be glad.'

The two girls started off together; Arden's slim figure, uncertain pace, charm of movement, contrasting with the rustic steadiness and straightness of her companion.

Susie looked up. 'We shall have wind,' she cried.

Then she picked a flower at her feet. 'And rain, I fear,' she added.

'Oh, I hope not!' said Arden.

'I hope not too; the corn's scarce turning yet in the shady fields; but there's marestails in the sky over yon, Miss Lawrance, to the windward, and see this pimpernel's closing before noon.'

'Dear me!' cried Arden, 'I shouldn't think it meant anything. What are marestails? Oh, those swathes of clouds? And that little red flower—is that your barometer?'

'You see it's so delicate, it shuts up at the damp air, just as the slug, there, comes out when he sniffs the rain.'

'Ugly little bestia!' Arden moved out of its way.

'Oh, Miss Lawrance!' Susie stooped down. 'I think he's so pretty. See, his shoulders are covered with a pattern, just like the carter's smock-frocks!'

'Still, I don't think he's pretty.'

They went on a little longer, Susie keeping close to the hedges and ditches.

'I'm looking for an orchid; I found one here once and never again—all green. I've got one pressed; but I never found another.'

'But what good would it be? A green thing's not pretty to look at, like a rose.'

'I've got a book at home,' said Susie, 'where I've pressed 'most every kind of flower to be found in these parts. You wouldn't believe what a many there are! Hundreds!'

'You should see the flowers in Italy!'

'If I could! Oh, there's more than flowers I want of Italy—books, pictures, history—things I can't have here. Still, there's a many good things in Arden, more than you know, Miss Lawrance.' She looked half-shrewdly, half-sweetly at Arden, as if she wished the girl to understand a liking she would not speak of; but in a moment she was off, her hands above her head, a Caryatide in cotton, searching among the tiny green plants and fern that grew in the damp interstices of the bricks of the bridge.

'Here!' she cried, 'look, Miss Lawrance, isn't it a lovely little fern? I've never found it before; but Mrs. Grubb, at the post-office (she's great in flowers, you know), she told me as sometimes it sprang here!'

Her eyes and one arm were still high up the wall, but, half-turning, she lowered the hand which held the tiny plant.

'Isn't it beautiful?' she asked.

'I think it's rather like the others,' said Arden. 'They're all alike, *Felce*; not much good except for doing up in bouquets.'

Susie's face fell a little. She privately thought it a little dull of Arden not to feel an interest in her plant; but her instincts of hero-worship immediately suggested that Arden, who had seen the greatest things of the world, could scarcely be expected to care for such very small ones. Still, she kept her plant, tying it carefully in her handkerchief.

'How still it is, and the sun so bright and yellow! There's a storm brewing.'

'How do you know?'

'Those are all signs. Hark! how loud the birds sing. D'ye hear? Yon's a blackbird. Fancy, at this season!'

'Do you know the birds by their voices?'

'Oh, yes, all of them. See, the swallows are gathering; I saw a Fare-thee-well-summer yesterday.'

'What's that?'

'A flower. It only comes when the swallows gather and the good weather's done.'

'Done! It seems to me we have never had any.'

'Oh Missie! Six fine days last week for the corn, and rain before and after for the roots; a spell of sunshine now, and we should have never such a harvest.'

'I don't care for the turnips; I care for the sun.'

Arden was not in a conciliatory mood: Susie perceived it.

'Of course you miss your home,' she said; 'you see, this is my home. I've always lived here—I've never known anything better. I would rather live here than anywhere in the world!'

'Is it possible!' cried Arden.

She began pouring out an incoherent eulogy of all the items that made up the world in which she had been happy—fitful-coloured olive-hills, white villas guarded by pointing cypresses, the great plain of the Campagna, the grey and lilac ridges of the Sabine range. Suddenly she stopped.

'There is the postman. Let us walk a little quicker.'

'Do you expect a letter?'

'Yes; from the Roses: from my old friends, from the people who would take me away.'

'Take you away! Would you be so glad to go?'

Arden, for all her hurry, stopped a moment; stopped with brilliant eyes and flushed cheeks, suddenly clouded with hesitation. Would she be glad to go? It was a question she had never asked herself. It seemed so sensible, so self-evident and necessary that she must be glad to go. What was there here she could regret to leave? What was there over there she did not long to look upon again?

Before she could put this thought into words, Susie, seizing her opportunity, had begun to speak.

'See, Miss Lawrance,' she began, 'I know you've had much to make you wretched-like since you've been among us. You came unhappy to a new place where the people of your own rank haven't been over-good to you, or hospitable at all.'

Arden blushed.

'I beg your pardon for speaking of it, Miss Lawrance, but plain words are best. And the old gentleman's been ill; you must have had a dull, lonely life of it up at the Bushes—no blame to them.'

Susie stopped a moment, but seeing the postman coming nearer and nearer she hurried on.

'You've had no one but us to know— farmer-people, and quite out of your station. See, Miss Lawrance, I understand why you should be glad to go. I didn't think of it before; but of course you looked on us much as you looked on th' 'emlock and th' apple-trees as you painted.'

'Oh, no!' said Arden, growing redder; but she felt it to be true.

'It was natural,' went on Susie, sadly, 'but all the time I've been thinking of you, and caring for you with real love.—

Don't speak, there's no need you should say anything—and if your friends call for you, go, dear Miss Lawrance, and be happier than you've been here. But if you stay——'

The girl stopped a moment to swallow something.

'Dear Susie!' whispered Arden, and took the girl's hand.

'If you stay,' went on the other, keeping hold of the little hand, 'there's something I have it on my mind to tell you. God knows I've no call to preach. But this isn't preaching, Miss Lawrance, it's only showing you something, as I showed you the little fern—and you needn't heed it any more than that, unless you like.'

'Go on,' said Arden.

'Well, Miss Lawrance, you don't like the country here; but you see to-day when the blackbird sang you didn't recognise it and scarcely heard it. You didn't see any meaning in the sky; you didn't understand what it meant when the beasts crowded under the trees, and the birds sang so loud, and the sunshine looked so yellow; you didn't know one flower from another, and scarcely saw a difference between them—now, did you, Miss Lawrance?'

'No,' said Arden; 'but I don't know what you mean.'

'You see,' explained the other girl, 'you find the country dreary just because you don't understand it, or recognise what's in it.'

'Yes?' queried Arden—'Well?'

'And don't you think, as you're so unhappy, it may be something the same with your life?'

'With my life?'

'With the old people up yonder, the country you're in, and all the things in the world you might do or care for——'

'I see—oh, how idle and ungrateful you think me!'

'I?—Nay, Miss Lawrance,' said Susie, making a not altogether unwelcome struggle to confess her hidden misery, lest Arden should look upon her as a preacher, a holy person; 'if I could tell you—as I can't—what sort of struggle and sin, all confused wrong and wretchedness, there is in my heart, you would know how good, and sweet, and pure, and calm, you seem to me—like a star in the dark, like a violet one doesn't look for in the lanes in January, a sort of earnest that there are better things in the world than those one just happens to have hold on—I'm not good—I can't tell you, but pray for me as an unhappy, miserable girl, who has lost the clue of right or wrong. Don't look so startled, dear Missie, I only wanted you to know how grateful I am to you for having come to see me now and again——'

'Dear Susie!' said Arden again.

'Thank you, thank you. And you will forgive me?'

'*Altro!*—I am grateful.'

'See—here's the postman!'

But there was no letter this day, either.

'You are very sorry?' said Susie.

'I—I don't quite know!'

Two or three days later she did know; two or three days later, when the desired letter came, long, kind, cordial, every phrase of it laden with allusions to the life she knew so well, the life of indolent, cultured people, familiar with all the great and beautiful places, with half the great or beautiful persons in Europe. How she longed for it again, the old, well-known, easy life! Suddenly she dropt the letter and began to cry.

'What's the matter, Sylvie, child?' asked her grandfather.

'Mrs. Rose is ill!'

'Poor thing—she's young too.'

'It's not that,' sobbed Arden; 'it's not dangerous, but they're going to Egypt for the winter.'

Poor child; she felt miserably forlorn and forsaken; at first nothing—not even her picture—seemed worth desire in life. And when her sobs calmed, and her mind grew more at ease, the thought that chiefly consoled her was not her yet unfinished picture, but the memory of Susie Williams' frank and loving face.

CHAPTER XIV.

IN THE HILL OF VENUS.

Soon after this time Arden finished her picture, and, accompanied by Mrs. Lawrance, drove into Warwick one fine afternoon and left her treasure with the frame-maker for despatch to the Birmingham Exhibition. Then there was nothing to do but to wait. The days went slowly by without event or record, while Arden wandered aimlessly about the garden, dreaming of her picture. As far as it went she knew it was good, and, though it didn't go very far, she thought it must succeed. Little did she dream how the shade of Baker would quiver with wrath over the daring greens, the uncertain breezy outlines of her work!

Now the picture was done with, it did not occur to her to visit the Farm save at rare intervals; and, indeed, she might have soon forgotten her friends there, and the course of her story might have run in different channels, but for the aching of a tooth. So small a thing may be the hinge of Fate! For so it was; Arden, roaming over-late about the fields, caught a severe cold in her face, which increased till the inflamed and angry fangs tortured her by day and night to the very verge of frenzy. On the third day she came down to breakfast haggard and wild. 'Where's the nearest dentist?' was her morning greeting.

'Law, Sylvie,' cried Mrs. Lawrance, 'how scared you look, poor child! It's all that wretched tooth; it'll tarrify you and tarrify you until you've had it drarn, mark my words.'

'Why didn't you tell me sooner, then?' cried Arden. 'But I'll go at once, to-day; I can't wait. Where does he live?'

'There's a dentist at Warwick, a surgeon-dentist as they call 'un, an 'ighly respectable practioner, so they say. But you can't have the 'orse to-day, Sylvie; gran'pa's lent him to Farmer Willis.'

'How can I go, then?' cried Arden, on the brink of tears; 'and I can't bear it any longer.'

'You might waäk to Henley, Sylvie, 'tis but a matter o' four or five miles; or Raynham, that's little better nor two miles aüf, and Tuke o' Raynham's an old established man.'

'Is he a dentist, too?' cried Arden, 'oh, that's all right.'

'Not, so to speak, a surgeon-dentist, I anticipate; but 'e's drarn many a tooth in our parish. Tuke's a chemist, Sylvie.'

Arden looked up. 'I'm desperate,' she said. 'If he can't do it, I'll go to the blacksmith and have it out with a pair of tongs!'

'Law, child, how precipitate you talk!'

cried Mrs. Lawrance, 'there's no call to be so wild; Tuke's a farmercuter, as they say; no mere Medical-hall of a man. He'll drar your tooth as well as a Birmingham operator; not as I'm saying I'd trust him with the stopping, leastways not gold; still, as for tooth-drawing, a strong wrist is all that's necessary, and no man alive could make a pleasure of it——'

'Oh, don't say any more!' implored Arden; 'I haven't the courage to stay, and soon I shan't have the courage to go.'

''Ere's your tea, Sylvie. Don't drink it while it's 'ot, and eat summat, child; it's exhaüstion makes you feel so vacillating and cranky.'

'Thank you.'

Mrs. Lawrance sat by for some time, looking kindly at the girl; at last she rose and pushed back her chair.

'Well, Sylvie,' she said, 'I wish I could accompany you this morning, I'm sure; but the bread's mixed and rising, and the butter's aäl got to be made up afore three; then there's the dinner——'

'Oh, never mind, Mrs. Lawrance,' cried Arden; 'I'm not afraid to go alone.'

'That's a good courage!' cried Mrs. Lawrance, approvingly. ''E'll put you out o' your misery in a few minutes, and I'll mince you some nice saft mutton for your dinner, Sylvie.'

The door closed and Arden was left alone.

To tell the honest truth, the poor child was at no time a heroine in her endurance of pain, and now, unnerved and prostrate, the idea of going alone to Raynham to a strange chemist to have her tooth drawn presented itself to her mind as little short of actual martyrdom. Courage!—she wanted nothing so much as to cry on some soft shoulder, while tender hands took care of her and loving words consoled her. But that was impossible. She sat still on her horsehair chair while sympathising Betty cleared away the breakfast, and remarked

on her melancholy looks. Arden had half
a mind to ask Mrs. Lawrance to send
Betty with her. But no; she would
deserve her step-grandmother's praises:
she would show herself of a good courage.
Suddenly the agonising dart and throb
of her tooth became so violent that
Arden rushed upstairs for her cloak and
hat; nothing could be so horrible as this.
She walked quickly through the village,
actually running when out of sight of the
houses, as nearly mad as sheer pain can
drive a poor helpless sufferer. At last she
saw Raynham, and began to walk, but still
quickly. The chemist's shop was at the
furthest end of the village; the door was
standing open.

'Can I see Mr. Tuke?' asked Arden
of a little lad playing in the doorway.

The lad looked up, alert and professional at once.

'Step in, Miss, take a seat, Miss,' he
said, moving a tall chair that overtopped

his curly pate. 'Mr. Tuke, Miss, he's gone out on business; customers, he said, were to wait: he wouldn't be long.'

Arden, panting and overheated, sat down, sick at heart, in the draughty shop. No wonder that her tooth began to rage in a veritable extravagance of pain. Nothing seemed worth hoping or fearing any longer: a dull endurance took possession of her. When, at an hour's end, the thin, dapper chemist re-entered his shop, he was confronted by a pale, sunken-eyed young woman, who could only point wildly to her face, who answered all his questions with an assurance that she couldn't speak.

Fortunately Mr. Tuke soon perceived what was the matter: nothing less than acute inflammation of the jaw. He would infinitely have preferred to send so responsible a case on to the dentist at Warwick; still it was clear that not a moment must be lost. A few exclamations of genuine sympathy and concern restored sufficient courage to Arden to enable her to sit down in the ominous leather chair and open as best she could her poor, swollen mouth. Then a grating, tearing sound; a jerk, the tooth had broken off—then another tug yet longer and stronger—the tooth was triumphantly extracted, but Arden— a senseless heap—lay crumpled on the floor without sign or breath of life.

It was an embarrassing moment for Mr. Tuke. In Arden's speechless condition, he had not learnt where she came from or who she was; and now she lay on the floor in a salvolatile-defying swoon. He bent over her and lifted her on to a table in the back shop, well out of the draught, placed a cushion under her head; loosed her gown, chafed her hands; but when a deep sigh seemed to reward his efforts, and when at last the heavy eyelashes were raised, it was but a moment ere the girl sank back into unconsciousness. The poor man was at his wits' end. An awful suspicion came over him that she might be a sufferer from heart-complaint, that syncope might end in death. A death in his shop; good Heavens! Mr. Tuke redoubled his efforts, and poured a glass of brandy, almost neat, down Arden's throat.

At last a faint colour struck up the whiteness of her cheeks; the little head, lost in the fallen yellow hair, began to stir uneasily upon the pillow. 'Thank God!' cried Mr. Tuke, and bent over the table to watch the return of life. And now a low moaning moved the purple lips, words followed; Mr. Tuke stooped to listen; he could not understand a word. She was alive, indeed, but a foreigner and delirious!

The poor fellow walked to the door and stood looking out in the street as if help might come to him thence and deliver him. The cool air fanned his forehead. He was just going to return to the inner room, when a fresh-sounding voice arrested him.

'Good day, Muster Tuke,' cried a fresh-looking man in a Whitechapel cart.

'Good day! good day, indeed!' cried the 'poor little chemist exasperated at this last insult of fortune. 'It's the very worst day I ever set eyes upon, that's what it is!'

'Why, what's the matter?' cried the other. 'Here; hold the horse, Teddy boy; I'm coming in.'

'I wish you would,' cried the little man, with an accent of testy relief. 'But is there anything I can do for you this morning, Mr. Williams?' he added with an instant resumption of his professional capacity.

'Let me see. Yes; there's an ounce of tartaric acid, a packet of carbonate of soda, a tooth-brush, and two penn'oth of camphor. Well! what's up this morning?'

'Just you come and see!' said Mr. Tuke in a hollow voice of mystery. He pushed open the glass-door, and there off the table flowed a stream of golden hair, which the dim light caught. The two men went in together; the girl was still moaning and restlessly shifting her head from side to side in half-unconscious, inarticulate pain. Her eyes were closed, her features drawn and wan.

'Good God! It's Miss Lawrance!' cried Harry Williams.

This was more than Tuke had dared to hope for—all responsibility was shifted off his hands. He began pouring the stream of his anxiety into Harry's listening ears; but Harry, who felt it profanation merely to stand and worship Arden as she lay there unconscious, could not endure the little chemist's eager talk.

'I say, Muster Tuke,' he said at last; 'I'm sure you've had your share of trouble. If you'll go and mind the shop, I'll watch by Miss Lawrance.'

'Very well,' said the little man; 'there's nothing particular to do—only when she comes round, you just step in and call me!'

And then the glass-door shut, and Harry Williams was left alone with his unconscious companion. It was a dull autumn morning, and in the back shop, with the yellow linen blind covering the one window there was little light. It seemed a very solemn place just then, that shady parlour, with its darkened window and outstretched moaning form of a beautiful woman. Harry sat down bewildered, oppressed. Through the door he could hear Teddy pounding something in a mortar, and the sharp, querulous amazement of the chemist's voice, as he recounted his adventure to some chance customer: 'and if Farmer Williams hadn't driven home from market round by Raynham, here I should have been saddled, may be, with a nameless corpse!'

But words and sounds alike seemed strangely far away, seemed to belong to another world than this dim, yellow-lighted room, where the white face, unconscious in its glory of hair, gave a solemn meaning to its commonplace surroundings. The dull flap of the blind against the open window, and Arden's dreary, sighing moans were the only sounds in the world that made a part of this moment. At last—it seemed after a very long while—Arden raised her head a little, and saw, dimly outlined against the window, the watching figure of a man.

'Papa!' she said, in a sweet, shrill, wandering voice.

Harry did not stir. The sweet voice went on:

'Oh, no. Papa's dead—papa's dead and gone. Is it Gerard that has come to fetch me?—Gerard?'

Harry turned sharp round; suddenly, unreasonably angry.

'No; it's me!' he said.

'A stranger!' cried Arden. 'Oh, where

am I? What's happened? What place is this?'

She sat up, leaning on her hand; her beautiful eyes wild and tired, her dress loose, her hair on her shoulders, her face still as white as death.

'Plague on me!' cried Harry Williams. 'I deserve as you shouldn't remember me, Miss Lawrance. I'm Susie's brother; and this place is Tuke's shop at Raynham, and you've been very faint, pore child—pore lady,—and I'm going to take you home.'

'Thank you,' said Arden, 'but I think I'm dying.'

Harry gave a little smile; his stepmother so often had said exactly the same thing.

'No, no,' he said caressingly as one speaks to a child; 'you're bad enough, pore child, but you're not dying. Tuke said I was to give you this.'

Arden put out a white little hand. 'You're very kind,' she said. 'I'm sorry to be such a trouble.'

'You're no trouble!' said Harry, with an emphasis that brought a little smile to Arden's wan face. She sat up and pushed her hair out of her eyes. Her glance fell upon her unfastened frock and fallen tresses.

'The servant girl's making you some tea,' said Harry. 'Shall she coom and 'elp you do your hair?'

'Thank you,' said Arden shyly.

'I'll send her, then.'

Harry walked out of the room into the little front shop, where the daylight, the orderliness of the scene, struck him as a surprise. Was it only an hour ago he had stopped Tuke in his doorway? He felt like Rip van Winkle; the world seemed immeasurably altered in that hour. Had he known the story, he might more truly have compared himself to Tannhäuser; for the chemist's back parlour had been his Hill of Venus.

CHAPTER XV.

A GOOD RESOLUTION.

An hour afterwards, Arden, wrapped from head to foot in Harry Williams' frieze overcoat, was sitting by his side in the Whitechapel cart, driving from Raynham to Arden. The chemist had made her promise not to open her mouth; so a little wan smile from time to time was all her share of the conversation. Harry spoke a little, chiefly about Susie and how ailing she had been of late; but he was thinking with a certain fierce wonder of the unknown Gerard whom Arden had called upon at waking. He had seen that she wore no ring on her left hand, and that sight had brought him a moment of acute consolation. Still there was much to be learned—much to be feared. Bah! what right had he, a mere coarse farming-man, to meddle with that beautiful angel's thoughts! He drove fast in a moody silence, until a soft little sigh from Arden caught his ears. He turned round and saw that she had gone very white.

'Don't let me faint!' she cried, putting out her hands, as if to keep off the oncoming blackness; but the life left her lips and her eyes shut. Harry put his arm round her to prevent her falling, and laid the drooping head upon his shoulder. He drove down the lane at a furious pace, the lifeless girl in his arms, and in his heart a sudden storm of passion, a fever of anxiety. They were still some little way from the village when the life came back into her face—and poor Arden, feeling very ill and wretched, began to cry like the tired child she was, the great tears rolling one after another down her face.

'Nay, nay!' cried Harry. 'You mustn't do that, Missie. We'll soon be home; only keep up your heart a little longer.'

'I—I haven't any home!' sobbed Arden.

'Pore child! Pore child! But see, that's our farm over yonder—'tis a good mile nearer than the Bushes. Stay there to-night, Miss Lawrance, dear, and Susie 'ull be so proud to take care of you.'

'No,' objected Arden; 'they'll expect me.'

'I'll go on and tell 'em,' said Harry; 'you'll be regular worn out. I declare I won't drive you any further.'

'Thank you, thank you,' sobbed Arden; 'you're really kind. I don't mean to cry, you know, only I can't help it.'

'Here we are,' said Harry, consolingly, as he turned into the clean bright farm-yard. 'Mother! Susie!'

It was very comforting to poor little

Arden to be taken possession of by friendly, gentle hands—to have all things settled with no reference to herself. In a few minutes a fire was blazing in the lavender-scented best bedroom, and she was lying wrapped in shawls, in a low chair-bedstead drawn to the hearth. A little table by her side held her cup and saucer, and a book, and by the window, Susie, as quiet as a mouse, was learning her French verbs by the fading light. Everything was home-like and easy and quiet. For some time Arden lay still, looking in the fire, and wishing she had not neglected Susie since the finishing of her picture. She was still weak and unstrung, and her own negligence and Susie's ready kindness both appeared very great affairs in her hazy consciousness.

'Susie!' she called at last.

Susie rose and came to the hearth, kneeling down by Arden's sofa.

'I don't think you're like the apples

and the hemlock, Susie. I think you're the kindest person in the world.'

'Like the apples, dear?' said Susie, fearing her friend was wandering in her speech.

'Yes—don't you remember? You said I only cared for you as I cared for the orchard. And then I didn't come and see you. But it wasn't that I didn't care—I was so miserable.'

'And are you worrying yourself about me?' cried Susie. 'Oh, my dear, beautiful little Princess Sylvia, I never expected you to care!'

'But I do,' said Arden softly, letting one small hand rest on Susie's shoulder.

'Thank you,' said Susie reverently; and for a long time she sat very still, neither moving nor speaking. At last she stirred.

'Miss Lawrance!' she said.

'Yes,' said Arden. 'I'm better.'

'Really better? Ah, yes, you look

more natural like, and your hands are warmer. Do you think you could bear to hear me tell you something?'

'Tell me something? Why, yes—of course.'

'It's not a story,' said Susie. 'It's quite true—it's dreadful. Oh, God, how can I ever have done it!'

'It's about you?' said Arden, anxiously.

'Ah, yes,' answered the other, 'more's the pity.'

She stopped for a little while and bent her head down into her knees.

'What is it, Susie dear?' said Arden. 'Please begin to tell me.'

'Yes, I must tell you, though I can't rightly judge whether I'm wrong in doing so; but when you said, dear Miss Lawrance, that you cared for me, I felt it was dishonest to hide it any longer.'

'Hide what?' queried Arden.

'Oh, me, the secret that's eating my heart out! I'm a miserable girl, and yet

I ought to be very happy, for Fred Masters loves me. But I've promised not to tell, and that's the harm of it.'

'Oh, Susie, poor little Susie!' cried Arden, sitting up on her sofa.

'I've been so miserable and so dishonest! Every time mother or Harry's done me a kindness while I've been so pettish and fractious, I've longed to ask them to strike me instead. Perhaps then I shouldn't feel so mean.'

'But why don't you tell them?' said Arden. 'It's very simple. Is your brother so *prepotente*?'

'So what?'

'Masterful, overbearing, such a tyrant?'

'Harry a tyrant!' cried Susie in amazement. 'Harry? Oh, he's the kindest and dearest to me of every one in the world. Why, when he was quite a lad, before I was born, he gave up his schooling to save father from the drink and all of us from ruin. If he's ever unmannerly, Miss Lawrance, it's because he's spent his life so for us and served us so—ever since he had sense to see what's right and what's wrong —that he's had no time to spend on himself. Harry a tyrant! Fancy! Why, the first thing I remember is his teaching me to walk; and he used to carry me round to all the beasts and teach me what they liked and what we kept 'em for. But you're looking tired.'

'No,' said Arden. 'Please go on.'

'Never was such a brother,' continued Susie. 'All the things he'd missed he made sure I should have—schooling, books, leisure, time to study every day. And when I was thirteen we lost some money in a bank, and there was some talk of my coming home from school at Stratford. Oh, how I cried! And Harry wouldn't hear of it; he said my education shouldn't go the same way as his, whatever happened. So he sent me back to school, and left off courting Rose King.'

'Oh, why did he do that?'

''Cause he couldn't afford to marry. Was'nt it fine?'

'But what did she think, poor girl?'

'Oh, she married Ned Swimburne. He went a courting her the same year.'

'Did Harry—your brother—did he miss her much?'

'I don't know. He never said so.'

'What was she like, this Rose?'

'Mrs. Swimburne, of Raynham? She's a good, comely, rosy-cheeked young woman with four little children who all look the same age, and a splendid dairy.'

'But how could you let him do it, Susie?'

'I don't know. Harry just said he'ld rather I went back to school; and I wanted to go, ever so.'

'He's a good brother. How could you keep a secret from him, Susie?'

'Ah! God only knows how hard it's been; and what's worse is that I know it's wrong.'

'Why don't you tell him at once—now?'

'Now; but I promised not?'

'Still, you told me.'

'True. Oh, dear Miss Lawrance, what shall I do, I wonder?'

'Of course,' said Arden, 'you must go and tell your brother!'

'But Fred——'

'A fig for Fred! he's not fit—— I beg your pardon, Susie.'

'Oh, I know Fred's not so fine a character as Harry; but that's all the more reason why he wants me; and he loves me; and I promised him.'

'Then tell him you retract your promise.'

'Then he would think I do not trust him.'

'Because you trust your brother! What nonsense! He's much more likely to think that if you deceive your people, you'll deceive him too. Your duty's clear.

'You're sure, Miss Lawrance?'

'Quite sure.'

'I believe you're in the right,' said Susie slowly.

'Well, and when will you tell him; your brother, I mean?'

'Next Sunday, the day after to-morrow,' said Susie.

'I wish you'd tell him now,' said Arden in her petulant, tired voice. 'I can't think why you wait so long.'

'Don't you see, Miss Lawrance,' explained Susie blushing, 'I only see Fred on Sunday mornings at the school, and it would be so mean to tell without giving him fair notice. Of course I could send for him and tell him, but I never would meet him in the week for his pleasure; and just to grant him a meeting now on purpose to tell him I won't keep my promise—that would seem meaner still, don't you understand.'

'I don't understand at all!' cried

Arden; 'the mean thing is to deceive your brother!'

'Ah, yes!' sighed Susie.

'And yet,' said Arden, afraid of striking too hard, 'I'm sure you're very good, Susie, all the same!'

'It doesn't seem much like it,' said Susie sadly; 'but now you must try and sleep a little, my dear.'

Arden dozed off into a happy rest; and, sitting silently by, Susie too was not unhappy; a great peace and quietude stole into her soul. She was no longer troubled by her fault, for she had determined to renounce it, even should that renunciation include her love. She would at all hazards do the right. But as yet she was free from the penalty of doing right; as yet she still could keep the dear, strange thought that, to the man she loved, she was supremely necessary. She had not been happy before; for her conscience had left her no peace. She might not be happy hereafter, for probably she would lose her lover. But for these few blessed, quiet intermediary hours she wore, as it were, her martyr's crown and her bridal wreath together.

Her peace was strangely little troubled by Arden's obvious contempt of her lover.

She herself owned that Fred was in the wrong; but already she was used to forgiving him. Moreover, in Susie's frank, outspoken rank of life, it was natural for unmarried girls to know what faults they might expect from their husbands. They looked for no ideals. Susie, for instance, high-principled Susie, was grieved but not surprised or shocked to know that her lover was sometimes the worse for drink. When she heard it she sighed, she did not blush. She had thought, with an admonitory heart-ache, that there would be so much the more pain and trouble in store for her. Susie's conception of marriage was strangely different from that of the girl who lay asleep by her side. Arden would look for love, and care, and mutual interests. Susie expected hard work, active management, responsibility, labour and pain, much discouragement, and possibly, in time, the sense that her husband blamed her for being old and faded. Yet the idea of shrinking from such a future did not suggest itself to her.

Some months ago Susie had done her best to dissuade a neat little dairymaid from marrying a drunken lout.

'You know he drinks, Nan!' she had said.

' 'Iss, Miss.'

' And he's fond of women.'

No answer, but a curtsey.

' And he's backbone lazy.'

' 'Iss, Miss, please, Miss. But if I har to 'ave him, I har.'

Susie had laughed, scolded, and pitied. It flashed across her, as she sat by Arden's side, that her own attitude was much the same.

CHAPTER XVI.

LOST AND FOUND.

Arden was delighted with the Farm. The simple, abundant, busy life, the quaint surroundings, the kindly, intelligent faces, had a dignity and position of their own. She did not feel so out of place here as in the slovenly semi-gentility of the Bushes. So, at least, she said to herself, prepared to see everything rosy in a place where she was so kindly treated. It was very sweet to Arden to be again a person of importance, a blessing and not a burden; in such a sentiment, vanity and gratitude shake hands.

She spent a happy morning, trotting after Susie round the dairy, so clean and fair, with its red tiles, and big yellow bowls of creamy milk; or round the farm-yard, where the turkeys struck her with dismay, and the downy yellow chickens with delight. There were two young calves and a litter of pigs. Arden clapped her hands with enjoyment, and was as pleased as a child.

Susie laughed, and petted her; but when Arden drew the likeness of the youngest calf, its soft uncertain legs in their baggy skin straddling under the weight of the thin body and large head, then Susie was all admiration. She did not know how to serve enough this fair, delicate girl, with her childish ways, her helpless orphaned sorrow, and the gifts and graces which appeared unmatchable in Susie's eyes. And Arden was well enough content to accept this lavish and headlong admiration. For that morning, she forgot to think of Rome.

Arden was easily persuaded to spend

that day at the Farm, and only return to the Bushes after church with Mrs. Lawrance on the morrow. There was much to do at the Farm. She filled all the flower-glasses, practised on the old piano, chattered to Harry Williams about the state of the crops, about Rome to Susie, and to Mrs. Williams about her tooth-ache.

They were all enchanted to listen; and by the end of dinner-time Arden considered them, save the Roses, the most intelligent people she knew.

She had not much sense of humour, or surely she must have laughed at the quaint juxtaposition. The Williamses, narrow, local, energetic, strong of mind and strong of nature. The Roses, cultured, shallow, cosmopolitan, familiar with a whole world of things the farmers of West Raynham never dreamed of.

For the people of West Raynham are of West Raynham; they are wise in crops and cattle; they take their politics on Sunday from the 'Birmingham News'; and their utmost idea of strangeness or romance is embodied in Guy Fawkes. The people of Rome are of Rome. They inherit three great civilisations, and claim acquaintance alike with Trajan, Sisto Quinto, and Victor Emanuel; they are the next-door neighbours of Michelangelo and Praxiteles; Nero and Seneca, the Borgias and Savonarola, have become familiar types to them; they have learned the wisdom in good and evil of the Italian Renaissance. Each set of people is, intrinsically, of equal value. The mistake is when those from Rome, going to West Raynham, look for Roman attributes there.

This is what Arden did. She did not perceive the real worth and character of her new friends; she did not enter, as at an opened door, into their different mode of life, and judge it by its own conditions. She did not so much as perceive that they were different. She liked them, and so she thought they resembled the other friends she also liked. She exaggerated their acquirements, and did not find out their character.

The afternoon swung by, and the two girls, who had been talking in the garden, came in to tea. Harry Williams was not in; and while Susie helped to lay the table, Arden, sitting on the settle, began to fill a quaint old punch-bowl with York and Lancaster Roses. The shadow cast by the high oaken back fell over her; she could not be seen save from the hearth.

'How late your brother is!' she said at last.

'Yes; most likely he's gone to Farmer Willis's about the harvest. He's the only man in Arden that has a proper "scarifyer."'

'A what?' cried Arden.

'A machine that rakes up the fallen

ears. I don't like it myself. I'd rather give the poor folk their leasing.'

'Oh, dear me!' said Arden; 'what lots of things there are I don't understand!'

'Poor little Princess! Well, I won't trouble you any more with the Farm. You can't be expected to take it in. Shall I sing while you finish your roses?'

'Please, Susie, if you will.'

Susie sat down to the piano, and, with a quaint little glance at Arden in her shadowy nook opposite, she struck into a fine old air—

>Who is Sylvia, who is she,
>That all our swains adore her?

The fine deep voice thrilled through the quiet room, where the fading daylight and the flickering brightness of the fire were contending together. The last level sun-rays fell on Susie as she sat in her light cotton gown, singing; her resolute head well poised; and now and then a fitful flame lit up, among the blackness of oak and shadows and mourning-clothes, Arden's sweet face and golden hair, her white swift hands moving among a lapful of gay striped roses. Suddenly the door was heavily flung open. Susie stopped her singing for a second, and smiled at her brother as he entered. But the smile died off her face, her cheeks whitened, and she sat still as stone, her hands upon the keys, quite rigid and grey; while Arden, bent over the flowers, saw nothing—was herself unseen.

The door swung to, and Harry came forward. He walked heavily, like an old man, with bent shoulders and sunk head.

'Stop your singing,' he said; and flung himself wearily down on the red-cushioned window-seat, huddled in his coat, his head in his hands bent down and hidden.

Then for a moment there was a dreadful silence in the room. It was not till some minutes after that he raised his head and spoke.

'Little maid,' he said, very gently; 'Susie!'

Susie rose. She knew what was coming.

'Come here,' he said; 'come here, Susie, and speak to thy brother.'

The girl went quietly across the room, and with a low cry she sank to the ground by her brother's side. He put his arm round her shoulder, and with the other hand he raised her face, and so for a long moment he sat, looking sadly into her hollow eyes.

'Susie, my girl,' he said at last; 'have I been a harsh brother to thee? Nay, answer me, dear; doan't cry. Why didn't you tell me, Susie, of your fine sweetheart?'

'I promised,' sobbed Susie; 'oh, dear, Harry!'

'You promised! And do words go for such a deal, Susie, and love for nothing? I never bad thee tell me of thy sweethearting, that's sure enough. I didn't think to deal with my sister like a cozening lawyer. Susie, there should ha' been no need of promises between us.'

'No,' said Susie. 'It was a lie, my silence.'

'A lie!' repeated her brother. 'Think how much it is, when we've trusted each other so! You've been my friend as well as my sister; and now—if you was a man, Susie, I'd turn you from my doors; but you poor women!'

'Oh, Harry, Harry!' sobbed the girl. 'Don't say it—don't be kind to me for that; oh! can't I ever make it right again?'

'No, Susie; what's done is done. You've acted a lie! and a lie's an unkéd thing between friends. I can't any longer think you the girl you was.

That's long gone by. There's an ugly blot on your soul, Susie; and, dearly as I love you, what can I say to the folk who make out you've kept your body no cleaner!'

'What?' cried the girl, starting up to her feet; 'what, Harry?'

'Down i' th' village,' said her brother, through his teeth, 'down there, they say as my sister's young Masters' mistress.'

'Ah!' cried the girl, clasping her hands across her face.

'They say cruel things,' he went on, 'a pack o' lies; but there's an ugly truth at the bottom. They say, down there, as you've met him at the school and at the church, regular, for weeks past; they say, Susie, as you made the worship of God a cloak for your sins and shameful secrets. And one coarse brute—I struck the lie down his throat before he saw me—swore, with a laugh, that he'd seen you kiss young Masters in the church.'

'That's true,' cried Susie, coming nearer.

'And if that's true,' shouted her brother, 'by God, it may all be true! and my only sister a common woman. Keep off!'

He pushed out his arm with a movement of disgust, and but for the high settle, which stood behind her, the girl would have fallen to the ground. As it was, she leant against it, sobbing in her throat, her head drooped forward, her hands twisted.

At this moment, Arden, who had been standing horror-struck and silent by the hearth, came rapidly forward; the end of her apron was twisted through her belt, and made a loose pouch still full of roses. 'Susie!' she cried, and ran to the choking girl; then, holding both her hands, she dragged her forwards with an impassioned movement.

'See, Mr. Williams,' she cried, 'it's Susie, Susie. Dare you doubt her?'

'I must,' groaned Harry.

'Last night,' went on Arden, with rapid speech and flashing eyes, 'she told me all—everything! my dear, brave, noble Susie! She told how she had been drawn into loving a weak, vain fellow, half from compassion and half from his gay, handsome face, and how, in a weak moment, she promised for his sake to keep it a secret. And how she fretted, and was miserable at deceiving you, and how she'd always loved you since she was a baby you taught to walk.'

'Doan't 'ee,' said Harry, quickly.

'And she told me,' persisted Arden, 'that she'd been tempted often to tell you, but she dared not break her promise until she was set free. And he wouldn't release her, the coward!—(be quiet, Susie). And at last she determined to break off her engagement if needs be, and tell you herself on Sunday—to-morrow. Oh, that she had told it one day sooner!'

Harry looked up. 'Go on,' he said.

'She waited till Sunday, you know,' Arden continued, 'because—and this you mustn't be angry at—she used to see Mr. Masters at the school, and never in the week. She never would see him any day or any time you wouldn't have heard of. Never!' said Arden, bending forward with Susie's hands still clasped in hers.

'Thank Heaven for that,' said Harry; 'she's not false all through then, liar though she be.'

'How can you say so?' cried Arden; 'one false step she made, and after that her very goodness led her on and on the wrong way. She wouldn't break her promise, though she oughtn't to have made it; and then, when she determined to tell you at all risks, she wouldn't take an advantage of her lover, and waited to tell him fairly first. She's done wrong, but she's not wicked.'

'Sylvia!' cried Susie, and loosing her hands from Arden's she flung her thin, wasted arms round the neck of her friend and lay, helpless and sobbing, on that kind, protecting shoulder. For one moment her brother looked on while Arden's tender hands soothed the trembling girl. Then he got up and stood in hesitation.

'Give her me,' he said at last. 'Give me back my sister! Susie, I was wrong, deceived; you're allus my dear good girl. Speak, little maid; speak, Susie!'

He took her gently in his arms. She lifted up her face, streaming with tears. 'But I love him, Harry,' she cried; 'don't think I consent to hate him! If he came into the house now I should know it. I should know if he was out in the lane. I should go to him and forgive him. You mustn't forgive me, Harry, until you know. I love——'

The words failed from her lips, and

her head fell back. Great sobs choked her utterance.

'Pore ! child,' said Harry. 'I know ; I know. Don't take on so, darling. My poor little sister, the worst is done with now!'

CHAPTER XVII.

FRIENDS.

POOR Susie lay, speechless and senseless, on her bed upstairs, with her mother watching beside her. She had now been ill for thirteen days with a low nervous fever, not dangerous but slow. It was perhaps the kindest thing that Fate could have sent her, releasing her from thought, and triply endearing her to the hearts of those she had wronged and wounded; so that now she lay quiet in a lethargy of weakness, while her future was decided for her. Downstairs, Arden, who had been persuaded to stay on and help Mrs. Williams in watching Susie, was talking to Harry. They were sitting on either side the hearth, deep in conversation, the broad-shouldered farmer in his shiny broadcloth, and the delicate, refined young girl: despite all difference, they talked like old friends, for favouring circumstances had brought them close together.

'I think she's better to-day, Mr. Williams,' Arden was saying, as she stooped towards the fire to see the colours of her crewel-work. She chose the proper strand, and threaded her needle. 'I shall have to go home again soon,' she went on.

Harry shuffled uneasily on his seat.

'It 'ull be hard work to spare you, Miss Lawrance.'

'Now that's very sweet,' said Arden; 'I'm sure at the Bushes they did not find it hard work at all. They were only too pleased!'

'I can't think it likely,' said Harry Williams.

'*Altro!*' cried Arden. 'But I can't bear them any grudge, for I have been as happy to stay as they were to spare me. I've been very happy here.'

'You're very good, I think,' said her companion. 'You've come into our house in our sore need, and made us happy in spite of it, and taken a share all the same as if you was one of us. If that's your happiness, Miss Lawrance, 'tis a blessed gift.' He spoke so seriously that the easy tears rose to Arden's eyes.

'Ah!' she cried, clasping her hands in her pretty foreign way, 'that's what I was dying for—to belong to some one, and take a share. In my grandfather's house I never was at home.'

Harry went very red. It seemed impossible that she could mean that she belonged to them, mere farmer people; that she found this house of his a home. He tried to look as though he had not heard, while the words sang and rang in his ears like a peal of wedding bells.

'And here, you see,' went on Arden,

'there really seemed a place for me. Oh, I never could forget that first morning when your mother, half distracted, kept asking poor, unconscious Susie where she had put the key of the linen-cupboard. Why is it that the saddest things make one laugh as much as one cries?'

'Do they?' said Harry, grimly. 'They make me wish to knock that villain down again, and harder nor the first time, too.'

'Do you know where he's gone?' Arden inquired.

'Not I, nor care, neither. He's a bad 'un wherever he may be; but I've done with him since he's gainsaid that wicked gossip as far as in him lay, and I did give him a good 'un in the eye,' Harry chuckled.

'I think you were quite excusable,' cried Arden. 'I don't blame you at all, for my part.'

'Blame me, Miss Lawrance? Why, I

couldn't ha' done less for my sister. I couldn't ha' done less.'

It seemed so comic to Arden, this favour of knocking out for one the teeth of one's lover, that she began to laugh, to the evident offence of her hearer. Country people are shy of being laughed at, and Harry was no exception to the rule. But after a moment he seemed to forgive her, regarding the pretty little figure with a pitying smile.

'You're so young,' he said; 'it comes handiest to you to laugh at all th' events of life. But 'tis pore work, pore work, laughing at men's villainies. And for the matter of that 'tis poor work enough wreaking one's anger on the scoundrel. Easy enough to knock him down and turn him out o' his parish; but, none the less, my dear little sister (so merry, so clever with her fingers as she used to be) is lying upstairs like a senseless log.'

Harry dropped his head between his hands, and stared gloomily into the fire.

'Hadn't it been for you, Miss Lawrance,' he went on, 'I think I should ha' been tempted to curse God; so awful was the blow. Fancy, in one hour to have all I most believed in changed to a deceit, a wicked cheat! I was a'most too dumbfoundered to be angry, even. Oh, I thought Susie 'ld ha' told me 'twas all a lie; but when she stood there, and let me say what I would and think what I would, without so much as a shake o' th' 'ead, I —I—oh, 'twas too much for me!'

'Don't think of it!' said Arden softly. She had left her seat, and was kneeling in front of the fire, warming her hands.

'Nay,' said Harry, looking down at the sweet face lit by the fire-flicker, 'nay, I'll rather think how, in the worst and thick of the trouble, you came forward, with them striped roses in your apron falling on the floor one by one. And your words was sweeter than any roses, red or white, for they gave me back my trust in little Susie;

nor any blessed angel out of heaven cudn't seem more marvellous-like to a man, or more full of pity and kind mercy, than you did then, Miss Lawrance, holding the little un' up in your arms till I cud take her back with a willing heart.'

Arden put out her hand. 'Thank you,' she said.

' 'Tis you, Missie, I must thank. I thought I'ld like you to know, that's all. But you're crying, I declare!' exclaimed Harry in dismay. 'What can I ha' done? What can I ha' said? Great orkerd brute I am.'

'Nothing,' said Arden; 'I'm quite happy. Only, you see, I'm—I'm not used to having any friends.' Harry stared. 'At least,' she went on, 'I've got three friends in Italy, only I don't know where they are. But that's so far away! I've got no friends here,' she said in a piercing tone.

'Oh, Missie!' said Harry Williams.

'Except you all,' went on Arden, 'all of you. Don't you see that's what I'm crying for?'

'Oh!' said Harry, blankly.

'Because,' explained Arden, 'I'm so glad. Because we are friends now, aren't we?'

'Miss Lawrance,' said the poor, bewildered farmer, 'if you'll have us for friends, as love and honour and thank you, and will do all our lives; if you'll take us for your humble friends, 'tis but like your sweetness and goodness. I can't say more.'

'Ah,' said Arden very softly, 'it's all settled then! We're friends now.'

They sat a little longer alone in the brown, dim parlour; but neither cared to say anything more after that. At last Arden went upstairs into the room where Susie was lying, so still and quiet. She sent Mrs. Williams downstairs and set herself by the white, peaceful bed. There was no sound, save now and then the yelp of the watch-dog, or the sleepy chirp of a half-awakened bird. Arden was happy. She was thinking how nice it was to be good, to be of some use in the world, and how natural it came to her when she was not crossed. This was the sort of life she had meant to lead when she left Italy behind; it was a sweet, noble life, she thought. She could not help feeling that she made a very picturesque figure in that troubled household; but her vanity was so innocent and artless that it only brought out the sweetest lines in her face—a wistful, yearning, devoted look. Just then Susie woke and turned round.

'Sylvia!' she whispered.

Arden bent over her and kissed her softly.

'Dear Sylvia,' said the weak, tired voice. 'I'm at peace now, at peace. You've saved me, Sylvia!'

CHAPTER XVIII.

THE LITTLE RIFT.

'Well, my dear Mrs. Masters, I am sure you will never repent of your generous decision.'

The Rector was standing in Mrs. Masters' drawing-room, rubbing his long white hands and smiling, as he prepared to take his leave.

'Don't go, Mr. Law,' said his hostess; ' or I shall think you came for nothing else but to wring a promise out of me!'

The Rector drew up a chair and sat down.

'It is seldom difficult to persuade you to generosity,' he said.

'I don't know about that,' answered

Mrs. Masters, drawing back her long neck with a quick, habitual bridle. 'I don't think I like being persuaded. But certainly I hate to do anything mean.'

'It will be a kind and delicate attention to go and see the poor girl. She has really behaved very well,' said Mr. Law, with an appeal in his voice.

'And Fred behaved very badly, you mean, I suppose? Poor Fred!' Mrs. Masters gave an impatient sigh. 'Well, I acknowledge she has turned out more reasonable than I expected.'

'I applaud her determination, for my part,' affirmed Mr. Law; 'unequal marriages are seldom fortunate.'

'He was regularly trapped into the engagement, I consider, poor boy!' cried Mrs. Masters. 'It was a most preposterous notion; but I won't quarrel with the girl, since she has given him up.'

'It must have been an effort to resign him,' said the sagacious Rector.

'It was, no doubt. Indeed, I should have gone to see her before—it was my natural impulse—but for the absurd scene that brother of hers made with my poor boy. I believe he considers it all his doing that I have sent Fred away for a while—out of his yellow-haired sister's clutches.'

'Well, well,' said the Rector, in his most deprecating voice; 'we are agreed that she has relaxed them.'

'Yes; and I have agreed to be magnanimous. But I shall expect a great deal of applause, I forewarn you.'

'You never cease to deserve it, my dear friend,' declared the Rector. 'But now I must go and see old Mrs. Barnes. I promised to be there by four.'

Mr. Law rose and took his leave, well pleased with his success; for he knew the most effectual answer to all village slanders would be for Fred's mother to call upon Susie. Now she had given her promise he knew she would not fail. But Mrs.

Masters chafed sorely against the bonds she had forged for herself, and from which there was no honourable escape. For a long time she wandered up and down her drawing-room like a wild creature in a cage. Oh, the hateful promise! It was too much to expect of her. She took up a book and threw it down again; began her work only to throw it aside. At last she rang the bell.

'Don't get the tea till five,' she ordered; 'I am going into the village.'

Thus it happened that on the last day of Arden's stay at the farm a loud knock was heard at the entrance door. Susie was lying on the sofa, still pale and weak; Arden had picked up the 'Siege of Dinant,' and was kneeling by the fire to catch the light on her page, while Farmer Williams, who had just come in from his turnip-fields, delivered a solemn warning, with inflammation of the eyes at the beginning and total blindness at the end of it. Arden laughed. Then came the knock at the door.

'Who can be there?' cried Susie. 'The carrier's gone by hours ago.'

'P'r'aps Mr. Law's stepped round,' suggested her brother.

'Oh, no, he came yesterday. I wonder if Betsy heard the bell. Yes. Why it's somebody coming in,' said Susie.

Arden dropped her book and rose to her feet; her cheeks, burned red by the fire, blushed to a deeper colour when she perceived the tall, handsome woman who entered the room.

'Mrs. Masters!' cried Susie, going very white.

'Yes, my dear,' said the great lady. 'Now pray don't excite yourself; lie still; I'm sure you are still very delicate.'

Susie couldn't answer, so many memories choked her throat.

Mrs. Masters went on, giving her time to recover: 'What a charming home you have here—really most picturesque, I declare! It would be quite a *trouvaille* to an artist, I assure you, quite a treasure-trove! It has been in your family a great many years, I think, Mr. Williams?'

'Two centuries and more,' growled Harry.

'Yes. No wonder you are proud of it. And how is your mother, Miss Williams?'

'I will go and tell your mother, Susie,' said Arden, glad of an excuse to escape. As she closed the door behind her she heard Mrs. Masters say—

'A relation of yours, I suppose.'

Somehow she felt very angry. She called Mrs. Williams, and then went upstairs to her own room.

A relation of the Williamses! Was that another insult of Mrs. Masters'? Arden looked in the glass. The neat foreign dress, the graceful figure, the refined face, were reassuring to see. She wondered what pleasure Mrs. Masters could find in persecuting her. Of course, she did not look like a relation of the Williamses. She began to smile a little bitterly as she contrasted her own image with Susie's Raynham frocks, and Mrs. Williams in her wonderful caps. 'Perhaps,' Arden thought, 'I have been wrong in letting myself drift into an intimacy with such people.'

The bare thought startled back her customary frame of mind. How silly she was to care what Mrs. Masters chose to fancy! The Williamses were her good friends, and she should know whom she liked. She would give Mrs. Masters no occasion for patronising her; that, at least, was certain. At this moment she heard Mrs. Williams calling her in the passage. 'I'm coming, dear Mrs. Williams!' cried Arden, and flew to the door. She had never noticed before how much like an upper servant the little woman looked.

'Is Mrs. Masters gone?' inquired Arden.

'Yes, Miss Lawrance,' said her hostess. 'And tea's ready if you'll come, Miss Lawrance.'

Arden ran down the staircase and flung herself on her knees by Susie's sofa.

'Oh, I'm so glad that woman is gone!' she cried. 'Hasn't she tired you to death, *poverina*, with her awful voice and her condescending manners; "*Non ragioniam' di lor, ma guarda e passa*."'

Arden sprang to her feet and struck an attitude. 'Really quite a *trouvaille*!' she exclaimed. 'Most picturesque, I'm sure.'

Though the farmer roared with delight at Arden's mimicry, Susie would not laugh. 'Now, that's ill-natured of you, Sylvie,' she cried. 'It was really kind of her to come and see me.'

'Maybe 'twas kind and maybe 'twas impertinent,' growled her brother. 'Leastways, I'm one with Miss Lawrance; I doan't like her.'

'Nor do I,' cried Arden. 'But she

thought Harry's speech had never sounded so broad before.

All tea-time, the quartette—usually so peaceable—seemed to be playing a game of cross-purposes; for Mrs. Williams, who thought the visit an immense honour and satisfaction, kept appealing for sympathy which Arden would not give.

'She's an odious woman!' she declared at last.

'La! Miss Lawrance, how you take my breath away!' cried little Mrs. Williams. 'Why, Mrs. Masters is a born Arden.'

'One would think you lived here under the feudal system!' cried the indignant girl.

'Well, Princess Sylvia,' said Susie, 'one may say there's never been a time when there hasn't been an Arden at the Hall and a Williams at the Farm. 'Tis natural we should feel our position.'

'*Mi da sui nervi!*' cried Arden, and jumping up from the table she went to the hearth and picked up her book. But she did not read; she felt that she had behaved ungraciously, and that is not a pleasant feeling for a saint and a heroine. At last she looked up and saw the farmer standing by her, looking at her with grave concern.

'I've been very rude,' cried Arden, with a charming gesture; 'will you excuse it for this once?'

'La! Miss Lawrance,' said Harry, 'there's nothing to overlook. Of course you're not used to know coarse, orkerd folk like us.'

Arden was immediately propitiated.

'Oh, yes, I am!' she cried, running to kiss Susie. 'You're my real friends, my only friends in England.'

She behaved so sweetly during the rest of the evening that no one guessed—not even she herself—of the little rift within the lute. It was her last night at the Farm.

The next morning she went to her

grandfather's house. The two old people did their best to welcome her; Mr. Lawrance tired himself with asking questions and telling old jokes, and Mrs. Lawrance got out her best quince marmalade for tea. But Arden missed the real gladness that her presence had called out at the Farm; she had, in fact, been made so much of there that the pathos and friendliness of this meagre little welcome home seemed quite flat and insignificant.

She sat quietly in her place at table.

'You're looking but poorly, child,' began Mrs. Lawrance, after a long and silent inspection. 'You're no credit to the Farm with them pale cheeks.'

'We'll freshen 'em up a bit, Nannie,' said the old gentleman. 'She's missed her drives, I'll warrant; they've got no pony carriage at Williams's.'

'Oh, they have,' cried Arden, 'a spring-cart, grandpapa, and such a nice fat old horse! I used to drive to Raynham nearly every day to fetch Susie's medicine from the chemist's.'

'Pore child,' said Mrs. Lawrance in her most commiserating drawl. 'I've never rightly forgiven myself that I let yer go to Tuke's alone.'

'Never mind,' said Arden. 'If you had taken me, I should never have gone to stay at the Farm.'

'Well, well,' old Mr. Lawrance began, 'I shall have to go and ask Mrs. Williams what weed they squirted on your eyes to make you so enchanted.'

'They were very glad to see me,' said Arden, simply; but the sentence had an unfortunate ring, and alas! Mrs. Lawrance was never wise in time.

'You can't say, Sylvie,' she began, in her plaintivest voice, 'as your grandpa's not been glad to see you, and I too, when you're amiable. But sometimes you are that fratchetty and discontented-like, I haven't it on my conscience to look pleased. But if you consider, as you appear to intimate, as we grudge you the bit of food——'

'I'm sure——' began Arden indignantly.

'Nay, nay, she didn't mean it, Nan; she said nought that was capable of giving offence,' put in the old gentleman. 'You're a good little girl, Sylvie, and we're both glad to see you about again, child.'

'Thank you, grandpa.'

'Just fetch me the big Shakespeare, there's a good girl. 'We're reading Hamlet in the evenings now.'

Arden fetched the book, and for an hour her grandfather's slow and husky voice was the only sound in the room, dim-lighted with the one candle, placed between her grandfather's book and Mrs. Lawrance's work-basket.

At last the act was finished, and the book put away.

'I've been thinking, dear,' said Mrs. Lawrance, stooping over her husband, 'as we 'aven't shown Sylvie that parcel the carrier braüt her yesterday.'

'All right, all right!' said the old gentleman; 'she can wait till the morning, I suppose!'

But Mrs. Lawrance had already opened the cupboard door, where Arden spied a high, narrow wooden case. It was her picture sent back from Birmingham.

CHAPTER XIX.

PIGSKIN WILL LAST.

Mr. Lawrance, quoting his favourite author, had often told his grandchild how misfortunes come, not as single spies, but in battalions; yet Arden, notwithstanding the rejection of her picture, was quite unprepared to defer still longer the hope of meeting her childish friends again. Her thoughts often turned to Gerard and Ellie, for she was not of a nature to forget, and the few impressions that her nature ever really received were very lasting. She had, therefore, been grieved when the Roses had left her so long without writing, and when, about a week after her return home, the postman brought her a letter from Cairo, she could hardly open it for the very nervousness of her eager pleasure.

At last she made up her mind to read the letter, and breaking open the envelope discovered the precious thin sheets; not quite as precious as they might have been, for they were written in Ellie's hand, but still a memorable feast for that hungry and fasting little heart.

She began to read—

'Shepherd's Hotel, Cairo.

'Dear Arden,—Yesterday's mail brought a whole sheaf of your letters, which had been lying at our Roman apartment until we could forward a reliable address. Gerard says you will think us very heartless; and mother asks me to send you a line at once, as she doesn't begin to get any stronger yet. I can't say I feel much like writing letters, for there is absolutely nothing to say. It is much pleasanter reading yours. I fear you are not having a good time at

your grandfather's place. It must be a
"one-horse consarn," as Daniel Willis used
to say. I should think even Daniel Willis
would be an enlivenment. Where do you
shop? You cannot get your clothes at
Warwick, I presume. They will send over
from the Bon Marché in the Rue du Bac;
but it is always a risk trusting to measurement. You may, however, be quite certain
of their gloves; they are excellent. It is
very different shopping here; the stores
are very dear, and I cannot say I ever feel
certain that their style is quite the latest
thing. One has a feeling that it was very
novel yesterday. I don't believe but you
might get something at Leamington. The
Sargents once spent a winter there. They
found it very dull; no theatre: all the
people hunt, for an excitement. They went
back to Boston the week before we left
Rome. Mollie sent you her affectionate
regards; she is grown very intellectual,
and has let her bang grow long. Well, I

can guess it is in anticipation of Boston. All this time I have not told you how we are. Mother coughs more than she used to do, I am afraid; but her spirits never run down; mine do, I must declare; one feels so outlandish here, and I don't believe I like having no *femme de chambre*. All the servants in the hotel are men and natives. Gerard says I am very parochial. We left Elise at Marseilles with her relations. Perhaps that is why I feel so dull. One can't have a good time with all the responsibilities of one's wardrobe hanging over one. It is awful to think how we shall get those trunks across the desert; we shall never do it in the world! Gerard is looking very well. He is quite devoted to sketching. The other day he met Miss De la Rue in a mosque; he is devoted to her also. Do you remember how he used to rave about her? But that was at Newport, before your time. Anyhow she used to snap her fingers at his ravings.

She has quite lost her looks, and is dying of consumption. I must say if I had to die I should like the complaint to bebecoming, or else I should not be on view to my admirers. We are going on to Syria after Christmas, to Mount Lebanon, Mount Hermon, the Mount of Olives, the Holy Land, the "entire figure," to quote Dan Willis again. I shall feel like crying for joy when I can look forward to going no further than down Beacon Street. I don't think I should love to live in Europe for a finality; but I suppose this is not Europe. Here we appear to be always on the go. If we survive the desert and the brigands, we shall be in Rome in May; then we are to stay a month with the Curtises at Pegli. I presume we shall go home *viâ* Leghorn; we would all prefer starting from Liverpool; but it depends on mother's health. If she is sick, she will go as much as possible by sea. I must say I shall think it hard if we do not spend a week or so in

Paris. Gerard said I was to tell you that if we stop in London, he shall run down to Arden and fetch you up to spend a day with us at our hotel. Does one say "down" or "up" to London? I know there is a superstition. Gerard would have put in a line but he is dining with the De la Rues. He is quite in the swim, and knows all the best people. I have to stay at home with mother. Gracious! what a long letter I have written; it is so difficult to stop when one has fairly got started off. I suppose I may as well stop here as anywhere else. Mother sends her kindest love, and I remain, dear Arden,

'Your ever affectionate friend,

'ELLIE.

'P.S.—I forgot to tell you we shall be at this address until New Year. After then our letters should be sent care of the U.S. Consul, Beyrout, Syria.'

Arden crunched the letter in her hand

with a certain feeling of indignation. Her long, frequent, tender letters, 'a whole sheaf of them,' had deserved something more than this frivolous reply. Perhaps she should have found some satisfaction in the well-meant and friendly little letter; but the starving beggar to whom you give a stone does not use it to stop a chink in his hovel wall: he is more likely to hurl it at your head. And Arden, usually so gentle and girlish, felt for a moment a passion of anger when she finished Ellie's epistle—the Rue du Bac, Mollie Sargent's fringe, Beacon Street! were these fit answers to her expressions of affection, her appeal for sympathy? So she asked her burning spirit, revolted at Ellie's lukewarmness. But she never repeated to herself that phrase concerning the fair Miss De la Rue; and yet this disaffection of Gerard's was perhaps the wounding point of the letter. Not that she had ever so much as fancied herself in love with him. But Gerard was her oldest friend, her special chum; she relied on him to remember her. And already it seemed he was so engrossed with newer friends that he could not spare the moment to send her a line of good wishes. And then the phrase floated up to her lips about the Roses' having known Miss De la Rue at Newport 'before your time.' Her time! It had begun when she was eight years old, nearly ten years ago. And now they could put off her desperate need, her hopes, her clinging affection, with stupid phrases about Daniel Willis and the difficulties of provincial shopping! But all the while that her lips blamed Ellie, her heart was sore with Gerard.

She seized her hat and rushed out of the house, with the letter still crumpled in her hand. She began walking quietly, as was her habit when greatly moved, up the orchard path into the hill meadow; there she sat down on the burnt grass on the brow of the rise, and, throwing off her hat, let the cool morning wind blow in her hair. The breeze, the large, simple view, the loneliness, enveloped her with a certain quiet. But she felt very sad, very deserted and desolate. She fell to thinking of old times, of her happy Roman childhood—oh, what would she not give to find the mere outside of it again! to hear the noise of the fountains in the streets, to see the endless steps of the Trinità dei Monti, with the branches of flowering trees, from the gardens behind, waving over the low brown walls, to hear the sweet voices of the nuns floating down it! She remembered the little ring her father had given her—it was on her finger to-day : the same, only a little worn and small ; as the love of Rome was in her heart. Her father had wished to leave Rome, the Roses had forgotten her easily enough. Was she the only person who cared to be constant? In her present frame of mind the fancy galled her. Henceforth she would care no more for her friends than they cared for her. And then there drifted out of the forgotten places of her memory Ellie's childish phrase about making friends of people passing through. Let them do it! Ah, she thought, they had always done it! She was, and had been, no more to them than Daniel Willis, Mollie Sargent, any chance amusing new-comer; and she had given them her very heart in exchange. She felt tricked, insulted, sore. She would no longer care for them; she would answer Ellie on her own terms.

'Miss Lawrance!' said a friendly voice from the gate.

She looked up; there stood Harry Williams, leaning over the rail and looking anxiously towards her. He seemed a sort of screen between her and the dreadful, wearying memory of the past. She jumped up and ran down the hill to the gate, and stood there; one hand with the letter in it held to her side, and the other reached out in friendly greeting.

'Oh, I am so glad to see you!' she cried. 'Come in and talk to me; I feel so lonely.'

She held the gate open with an inviting smile, and of course the hapless farmer entered.

It was indeed a wonderful moment for him. He had missed Arden sorely; his home had seemed but a sunless place without that glancing presence. All the force of a dogged and obstinate nature he had centred on her as its prize, all the passionate devotion of his heart. He had never seen any one like her. She was so good, so beautiful, so sweet and friendless. And yet—even while he longed to protect and champion her—to shower all manner of love and service upon her—he never lost sight of the barrier between them, the barrier of rank and position which, from his standpoint, it appeared impossible to overleap. His father had married above him indeed, but not a lady like Arden, who was the loveliest lady he had ever seen. He had expected when he saw her again that she would have drifted further apart from him, now that she was out of his house and had returned to the company of her own people. But instead she had flown to him like a bird to its nest—had run to him with open arms. Poor Harry, ignorant of the truth and putting the most favourable construction on Arden's welcome, was wandering in a Fool's Paradise of delight. Although he loved her so dearly, he felt an acute thrill of joy when he realised her lonely and friendless life. She might come to him so for warmth and shelter; would not he gladly spend the dearest forces of his heart in her defence and service?

All this while these two persons, thinking so differently, were strolling side by side up the steep rise of the meadow. Arden, who was weary of her thoughts, so much less sweet than her companion's, broke the silence.

'This isn't like *your* pastures, Mr. Williams,' she began, smiling in his face and thrusting the little point of her shoe into one of the great fissures in the turf.

' 'Tain't in very good condition,' assented Harry, too much engrossed with the smile and the foot to care very much about the land.

'What should you do with it if it were yours?' inquired Arden.

'If t'wur mine?' said Harry, with a look of bewildered, impossible gladness. 'Oh, the land you mean?'

'Of course,' said Arden. 'What should you do?'

'Well, you see, Miss Lawrance, this land's in reg'lar bad condition. I should turn it up and drain it and drench it with good manure—them Brummagem oyster-shells 'ud do, button-waste and stuff—and so I should let it lay fallow for a season; potatoes then 'ud be the most likely thing, and the next year t'wud be fit for cereals and roots, or you cud lay it down in grass for the dairy.'

'I wish it *were* yours!' cried Arden: 'it's a pity to see everything falling into rack and ruin for want of a little care.'

'And so you wish t'wur mine,' said Harry, more than ever charmed. 'I wonder what th' attorneys 'ud make of you, Miss Lawrance?'

'I'm afraid no one would make much of me,' cried Arden. 'I'm a failure!'

Harry began to laugh; but, seeing that she really looked sad and almost bitter, he stopped and gazed at her anxiously.

'D'ye think so?' he said very gently. 'You mustn't give way like that, Missie: 'tis only that you're moped and moithered up at the Bushes, with the old gentleman so ill, and Mrs. Lawrance——'

He stopped short.

Arden began to laugh. 'Oh, it isn't only that!' she cried, and then Harry saw the letter crumpled in her hand.

'Bad news!' he said. 'Pore child, I'm sorry.'

'Yes,' replied Arden, touched by his concern, 'it is bad news, although no one's dead, or ill, or anything of that sort.' She glanced up at him. He looked so kind that she went on; 'but, you see, these are my very oldest friends—my very oldest—and they seem to have forgotten all about me already. It's very soon!' said Arden, with tears in her voice.

'Brutes!' ejaculated Harry, clenching his fist.

'No,' said Arden, 'they're awfully nice so long as you're there. Every one—and they most of all—used to be so sweet to me. And now not one—not one—remembers me.'

Harry did not speak at first, but as she waited he burst out :

'I'ld like to punish 'em, I would!'

Arden smiled. She had felt so weak and desolate that this ferocious championship was welcome to her.

'We won't punish them,' she said, with a wan smile, 'we'll forget them!'

'T'aint so easy forgetting,' said Harry, carried out of himself by her appeal to his sympathy. 'Haven't I tried by day and night to forget thy sweet little face by my hearth and thy clear voice in my ears?— And all no use, no use.'

Arden looked up frightened. 'Mr. Williams!' she cried.

'Yes—me—Williams,' he went on, with a moment of passionate self-assertion; 'look down on me as much as you like. No doubt you'll niver speak to me again. But love is stronger than many waters as I've read in the Bible, and though I know I'm a fool—an uplifted, foolish dreamer—I've dared to love you, dear. How cud I help it?'

Arden said nothing.

'How cud I keep thinking,' he went on, 'as you're a lady born and I a rough orkerd lout of a farmer, when I found you lying senseless in Tuke's little parlour; and when I took you home, so childish and frightened-like as you wur; and then when you came out like an angel and gave me Susie back? How cud I help it, Miss Lawrance, think of that.'

'Yes,' said Arden timidly.

'Not as ever I hoped, in my sober senses, as I cud be more to you than Susie's brother. But, for all that, the thought of you is allus with me. I get no peace by day and night. Oh, God, how hard it is that I should be so different!'

'Don't,' said Arden, laying a light little hand on his arm, for his passion was piteous to witness.

'It must be so!' said the farmer more

calmly. 'I must just look on, I suppose, while they slight you and moither you to death. But if ever you want summat as I can do, Missie, you'll remember I'm allus there.'

'Thank you,' said Arden.

'And you woan't be hard on Susie? Poor child, 'tis not her fault, and she fair worships you, Miss Lawrance. I'll keep out of your sight. I'll not trouble you any more, I promise. But you woan't remember it agen the little 'un?'

'No,' said Arden.

'I'll leave you now then, Miss Lawrance. Forgive me if I've taken a liberty as frightens you. 'Twoan't happen agen. Good-bye.'

'Oh, I'm so sorry!' cried Arden.

'Nay, doan't 'ee be sorry; my life's the sweeter to me, as well as bitterer. I'll be a better man for't henceforrard. I'll keep the memory of your sweet goodness in my heart, and I woan't be so hard to them as have wronged me. But now I'll leave you, Missie. Good-bye.'

He turned slowly round, without reaching out his hand.

'Stay,' cried Arden. 'I don't think I want you to leave me!'

CHAPTER XX.

I'LL LOVE YOU TRUE.

An hour afterwards Arden was upstairs, safe in her room at the Bushes. As yet she did not realise the promise she had made; she did not understand all that she had implied when she had told her lover that he might stay—that she would accept his love and service. She had not promised to love him. She had told him to wait and hope. She felt frightened now; she would willingly draw back. And yet she was proud that so strong a heart should own her sway. To do her justice Arden did not think, in that moment, of the difference of rank between her lover and herself. In that hour of fear and hope, and bashful new-born passion, she merely was a woman and he a man; she the defenceless, he the would-be lord and servant and protector. She feared, not to condescend, but to surrender.

This mood passed, and Arden grew aware that her lover was a squire of low degree: that he did not look or speak or think the same as, for instance, Gerard Rose. But in her present soreness of heart the difference was welcome. Let go the conventional polish and the shallow smoothness, cried her spirit; choose the substantial worth plain and solid. She wanted a refuge from herself, and from the world, and Harry was strong and kind and sure. Nor did Arden realise to the full how much lower than hers was his social and intellectual platform. She had lived so little in England, knew absolutely nothing of English society. The English she had known were birds of passage, all alike in the boarding-house equality of Brown and

Brabazon. They were all foreign names to her, Williams as good as Arden; and the language too was foreign. She did not think the 'dialect,' as she called it, a stamp of commonness; the difference between the tongue of an Albizzi of Florence and a Borghese of Rome, between the people of Milan and the people of Naples, was as marked as the difference between the speech of Harry Williams and of Gerard Rose. Of course he was only a farmer. But Arden's imagination was impressed by the picturesque roominess of the old Farm in which his family had lived for more than two hundred years in homely plenty and comfort. Among the Americans she had known, travelled and cultured *nouveaux riches*, among the painters and singers living here and there, wherever a studio was good and cheap, such a thing was impossible. She found the idea full of dignity, of repose. She would be glad of such a resting-place.

She sat quiet, trying to think, and ever finding her thoughts float off into a dream, until the little servant came to call her to dinner. And when she went down she said nothing about the things which had happened that morning. They seemed, indeed, unreal. But as she sat quiet afterwards, in the dusk, she heard a sudden ring at the bell and Harry's voice in the hall. So it was to be all made known, it was neither a secret nor a dream! She started up to make her escape, but the door opened and Harry took her hand.

'I want you to stay and listen, Sylvie,' he said.

Mr. Lawrance, asleep in the great old velvet chair, started out of his doze and looked round him.

'What, Williams?' he began, 'so you've come to see my little girl. Very kind of you, I'm sure, very kind! She never stops telling us of all the charms and wonders of the Farm.'

Mr. Lawrance was quite awake now. He looked, Arden thought, more dignified and impressive than she had ever seen him; there appeared a difference she never had noticed before between the old gentleman, urbane and condescending, in his rumpled old clothes, and the high-coloured black-haired farmer in his glossy broadcloth and blue tie, awkwardly smiling through a blush, as he twisted the brim of his hat in his hands. She wished it were over, settled, either way.

'Mr. Williams has come to see you, grandpapa, not me,' she said.

'Eh?' cried the old gentleman, 'come to see me, has he? Anything wrong with the fences again, Mr. Williams?'

'No, Mr. Lawrance. Not as I know of,' said Harry sheepishly. 'I've made bold to mend them rails in the Five Acre. But it's not of such every-day business as I be come to speak.'

Arden blushed. 'I think I'll go,' she said.

'Nay, Sylvie, wait a bit,' cried her lover. 'Mr. Lawrance, doan't you see what's up? I've come to ask you if I may see Miss Sylvie to pay her my addresses-like. I know it is a bold thing for the likes of me to love her; but I do!'

'Dear me!' cried Mr. Lawrance, settling his spectacles to look the better at the young farmer, 'this is very unexpected—very. I really can't commit myself to an opinion.'

'No wonder,' said Harry, 'as you should think me uplifted. So I be; so I be. But I doan't want Missie here to pledge herself to anything. 'Tis only a chance to make her bear with me as I ask for. She's free as air, Mr. Lawrance; and if she doan't grow fond of me by-and-by there's no occasion as she should go any further. 'Tis a wife I want, not a slave.'

Arden looked up. She liked to see him so, bold and modest.

'Well, well, Sylvie,' said her grandfather, 'I suppose you must go your own gait; I can't interfere. But I can't imagine you a farmer's wife, child.'

'There's no call, Mr. Lawrance, as you should fancy her any different. I cud keep my wife like a lady, I'm proud to say. She'ld never have to sile her white little hands with looking arter the beasts, I'll warrant you. She could set all day in the best parlour on the sofa and read her book. She shud have everything she set her heart on, and never do a stroak o' work from morn till eve. I'm a rich man now, Mr. Lawrance. I've nigh a couple of hunderd acres of land as turns me in a good fairish profit come fine seasons and come foul. I'm not so poor as my wife should break her back with housework.'

'Yes, yes,' said Mr. Lawrance; 'but some one must look after the house!'

'There's Susie,' ventured the eager

lover, 'as knows every stock and stone in th' old place, as 'ud be proud to stay on and see arter the managing o' things. I've got a little house in Wood Lane as she cud live in with my mother, and come backards and forrards every day, or they cud stay on, just as Sylvie likes. No need to think of the work, Mr. Lawrance; there's many an old woman in Arden as 'ud jump for joy to come and manage for us for twelve pound a year and her keep. There's a plenty of old women, but there's only one Sylvie as ever I set eyes on.'

'I don't say no,' said Mr. Lawrance, 'and I don't say yes. The fact is, it is not in the pale of my jurisdiction; not in the pale of—— Do you love him, Sylvie?'

Arden started.

'Oh, Sylvie!' cried her lover, 'I doan't ask thee to love me. Bear with me, dear, and let me stand up for thee and take care of thee, and have the thought and love of thee allus in my heart. It's a great sacrifice, Sylvie, to bid you make for the likes of me. But you're loanly, Sylvie, here, and I'm loanly; and I'd love you true and firm till death do us part.'

'That's so long,' cried Arden, with a little shudder. 'What shall I do? What shall I say?'

'Pore child!' cried Harry. 'You look in a maze, like, with doubt and wonder. Doan't you get frabbing over me, Sylvie. I'd like to save you trouble and not to saddle you with it. If you'd trust me, if you'd only trust me, I'd so smooth and soften things for your resting on 'em. But now I'll not take up your time, Muster Lawrance. Like enough you're busy this harvesting time, only I thought it best to be plain and straightforrard.'

Arden looked on while Harry and her grandfather made their brief adieux. She did not go out to the door with Harry, but ran up to her own room. There she thought to unravel the tangled skein of her heart; but, weary and tired, she fell asleep in the straight-backed red armchair by the hearth. She slept long and deep, and dreamed sweetly—dreamed of Rome, of Gerard and Ellie, of her father, and Mr. Rose, with his thin face and hollow voice. Then she woke with a start, for she dreamed she had strayed away from her companions and was lost, alone, in the chill, grey shadow of the ilex-trees.

CHAPTER XXI.

WOO'D, MARRIED, AND A'.

It was all settled at the apple-gathering Susie had pressed her friend to come to, so Arden laid her doubts and fears aside, and left the chill and narrow kindness of her home to find light, warmth, merriment, and welcome at the Farm. It was a beautiful September day, warm and sunny. On the orchard that Arden had painted, the sun shed its mellowest rays, and the grass was all flecked and streaked with light. There were ladders set against the trees, and the men lying along the boughs tumbled the red and yellow fruit into baskets that the women held up beneath. It was while Arden was holding up a great osier basket for the apples that Harry in the tree sent pelting down, that she determined to leave her dull, vacant home, and make a part of this busy, happy household. 'If he should ask me again,' Arden thought; and before their work was finished he had asked and she had consented.

She did not regret it that evening when, as they all sat roasting apples round the fire, Harry told his mother and sister. The pride and delighted incredulity of Mrs. Williams sweetly flattered the poor lonely girl, who had of late grown drearily accustomed to find herself merely a stranger in the way. And Susie flung her arms round her new sister's neck in a burst of grateful affection. Harry was kind, too, and gently considerate, asking her questions about her old foreign life, and never plaguing her with the newer claims of his devotion. She was left free to become at home in her new house, simply and without demonstration. And though, when at last she rose to leave, her cheeks were wet, for she had been talking of her father, she was not unhappy. It was pleasant to belong to somebody, to have rights and duties and a place in the world again.

She was not, indeed, 'in love' with Harry as she had known some of her friends to be in love. On the other hand, she cared for him very much more than certain other friends cared for their husbands, who had been held to make brilliant marriages. Arden, brought up with somewhat foreign notions, considered herself quite sufficiently devoted. She had a great trust in Harry; a quiet, reliant affection. She liked him to take care of her; it pleased her to see the hold she had upon him; and though she did not see him very often, she was sorry when he went away.

Yet she certainly did not wish for an everlasting *tête-à-tête*. She used all her influence to persuade Mrs. Williams and Susie to stay on in the old home. And so it was arranged; but the best parlour, locked up for years, was refurnished as a special sitting-room for Arden. It was a large, light, pleasant room on the opposite side of the passage to the common parlour and higher than that, for to get to it you went up a little flight of steps. The wainscot was painted apple-blossom colour; the hangings were all of white holland, and the chairs and the new sofa were covered with it. John Lawrance's pictures hung on the walls; and there was a bookcase full of books which Arden had chosen in Leamington; and her guitar hung by a red ribbon from the wall. The windows were filled with geraniums and fuchsias. It looked like the bower of a bride.

A little staircase with a carved rail led to a big bedroom above, which, like the sitting-room, had another door leading on to the landing; so that the occupant of these two rooms could be sociable or retired, as fancy prompted. These were to be Arden's special share of the house.

In October they were married. It was a quiet wedding, one Sunday morning before the service began. Mrs. Williams would indeed have liked to make a show—it was not every farmer's wife whose stepson connected himself with the quality!—but Arden pleaded her recent loss, and of course she had her way. So one Sunday she drove to church, with Mr. and Mrs. Lawrance, closely wrapped in furs, which left no ruching visible of the short gown of white satin underneath; and at the church door she met her bridegroom, Susie her bridesmaid, and Mrs. Williams all a flutter with ribbons and ostrich tips. Her grandfather gave her away; and scarcely did she understand the step she had taken before the brief service was over, and she was Farmer Williams' wife.

They passed down the fast-filling

church, where eager hands outstretched from every pew greeted the bridal pair, while hearty voices blessed them. And every voice said something kind of Harry. He strode down the aisle erect and proud, with shining eyes.

'I have to keep nudging myself to feel it's true,' he whispered to his silent little bride.

At last the shaking of hands was done, and the voices came to an end. Then the little wedding procession stepped up to the sunny churchyard. A rank of school-children, to whom Mr. Law had given some late roses and chrysanthemums, stood in the porch of the church; and as the bride and bridegroom came up the steps from the aisle below, they threw their flowers with a hearty will, pelting them with sweet and bitter blossoms. One caught in the lace at Arden's breast; it was a blood-red chrysanthemum, fair to see, but with the smell of wormwood.

She smiled at the children and stuck the flower in her bodice as she stepped out where the October sunshine lay like palest gold over the mounded graves. It fell, too, on her white dress and sweet, smiling face.

"'Appy the braïde the sun shaïnes on!" shouted the children; and Harry pressed the little hand that lay so lightly on his arm.

So they were married, and all her struggles over. At first the bird beats wildly against the strange, confining bars, but soon it is reconciled and makes of the cage a home. It is true that not only singing nightingales, but even chirping robins, die in confinement; but there are many more that live—linnets, canaries, thrushes, blackbirds, even the wild and soaring lark. So that the chances are for happiness. And Arden surely might be happy now that in this cold foreign land she had found a love that was warm and familiar, to be hers till death. Poor little frozen bird, unable to find food or shelter in the winter nights, surely the comfortable cage stored with grain and wool will be a happier world for its piteous helplessness!

When the wedding breakfast was over and Harry and his bride had left the Bushes for their honeymoon at Leamington, Susie and her mother took their leave and walked home together. Mrs. Williams was full of conversation. Mrs. Lawrance's moulds and made dishes, the cut glass and dessert knives, the Venetian decanters and Faïence fruit dishes (which John had given his mother years before), filled her soul with wonder and envy. At the same time there was an absence of solid fare which she could not justify to herself on such an auspicious occasion; and Susie had to listen to many *pros* and *cons*, as she walked wearily home. She was very tired and still weak from her illness, and sad thoughts of her own frustrated love would keep breaking through the talk of Harry's wedding. It was an effort to answer her mother's merry chatter; but the effort braced her heart and did her good.

'I wonder now,' said Mrs. Williams, 'where they got the notion of them chicken-patties from? They were very genteel.'

'You might ask Mrs. Lawrance,' suggested Susie.

'So I might. I suppose, the two houses being connected.' Mrs. Williams bridled a little. 'Although I can't quite say I approved of having no substantial victuals. What do you think, Susie?'

'Well, it was very early, mother dear.'

'Of course,' rejoined the elder lady. 'But in my young days—and you know I used to move in very genteel society before I married your dear papa—in my young days, as I was saying, a wedding breakfast was always quite a solid meal.'

'Perhaps the fashion's changed,' put in Susie.

'May be,' replied her mother doubtfully; 'perhaps; but what muddles me is this. One never knows, concerning the way they carry on at the Bushes, how much of it comes from Mr. Lawrance being a quality-man, and how much from his wife being a servant-like, as one might say.'

'It is puzzling, I suppose,' assented Susie. 'You might ask Sylvie which is the correct fashion.'

'Ay, so I might, Susie!' cried her mother. 'That's certain, Sylvie's a real lady—quite *distinguée*, as we used to say at school. Every inch a lady she is, the dear child.'

'And so good, too!' cried Susie; 'so sweet and kind and helpful. I'm sure I thank God every night for having sent her to us!'

'It 'ull be a comfort,' said Mrs. Williams, 'to have her always in the house.

Many's the time I've wanted some one to give me a hint about my caps and dresses.'

'I'm sure you couldn't look nicer, mother,' cried Susie, gazing with admiring eyes at the odd little flibberty-gibbet at her side.

'That's all very well,' said her mother 'but there's a different *cashy* about Sylvie's things. We shall do matters now in a very different style, and get into quite another set, no doubt.'

'We can't desert our old friends,' cried the girl.

'Who talked about desarting, Susie?' said her mother severely. 'They mustn't be presooming, that's all. I can't have the Kings and the Willises forced down Sylvie's throat.'

Susie said nothing.

'You see,' her mother went on, 'she will naterally want things done in the way she's always been accustomed to. I must give Harry a hint about his boots; 'tisn't decent of him to come to tea so muddy. She'll have quite a genteel influence over him, no doubt, and I'm sure there's room for improvement. I'm quite longing, Susie, as you should get married too—so nice as we'ld manage the wedding!'

'Oh, mother,' said Susie in a hushed hurt whisper, 'you know that can never be!'

'And why not, I should like to know? Now don't tell me you can't forget him—nasty, low-minded fellow—or I shall say you have no proper pride. Of course I don't mean you to marry young Warner. I should always say No, if I was you, to the likes of him. But Sylvie has plenty of acquaintances among the gentry—she said as much herself—and a nod's as good as a wink to a blind horse——'

Mrs. Williams gradually stopped her harangue, conjuring up a golden future, in which Susie was married to a foreign Count with ardent black eyes and a thrilling tenor voice. Mrs. Williams—who prided herself upon her freedom from insular prejudices—was so elated at the distinction of this idea that she had not half exhausted its resources when she reached her own gate. She did not notice it and was going further on, when Susie stopped her.

'Why, here we are, mother!' she cried.

'We shall see what we shall see,' replied Mrs. Williams oracularly.

There was plenty to do during the bride and bridegroom's absence; for neither Susie nor her mother would have been happy, had not everything in the house shone and glistened as brightly as they hoped their Sylvie's future might. They gave themselves little rest from their endeavours; washing all the prettiest, long-treasured china for Arden's rooms, and filling the bowls with pot-pourri; transferring all her treasures from the Bushes to her new home; unpacking her things, and laying them neatly in her drawers, between sprigs of lemon-plant and lavender, that she might find all ready to her hand, and feel herself indeed at home. There was great business in the kitchen, also: plum-puddings and mincemeat to make, and a grand baking of cakes and dainties. When the last day of the honeymoon was over, there was still so much to finish that Susie rose long, long before the wintering sun began to shine. A final polish was given to all the brass and woodwork, a final daintiness to Arden's quarters; the few rare flowers that grew in the sheltered kitchen window were plucked and put in water on her table; immense fires blazed in the grates; the easiest chair was drawn to the hearth. At last, the spring-cart was sent to the station; it would hold but two, so Curtis was despatched with it, with orders to walk home; and then, there being no speck or dimness left throughout the house,

Susie and her mother went upstairs to make themselves as orderly. Susie, even, had scarcely finished her swift adornment, before she spied the cart coming down the lane, at a great pace. 'How glad they are to get home!' she cried. In another moment, the whole household was at the door.

'Welcome, my daughter Sylvie!' cried little Mrs. Williams, with tears in her eyes. The cart stopped; Harry sprang down, and lifted out his bride. But could that be Sylvie—that pale, listless, weary girl, who smiled wanly at them, and walked, without a word of thanks, into the room they had made so beautiful for her? She sank into the great chair with a weary sigh; and they all stood looking at her—Harry, beseeching and hurt; Mrs. Williams, amazed past all belief; Susie, with tender kindness and concern. But Arden did not look up. 'Oh, I am so tired!' she sighed at last;

and her head fell back against the chair. Susie came forward quietly. 'That's it,' she cried; 'she's tired out. Go away, you foolish people, and get her some tea, instead of wanting to kiss her. I'll see to that.'

'La, Susie!' ejaculated Mrs. Williams; but she took Harry's arm, and walked out of the door which Susie held open for them with a show of mock imperiousness. But, once the door was shut, the girl dropped her pretty airs, and ran to Arden's side.

'What is it, my darling—what have they done to you, my sweet Princess Sylvie?' she cried, as she dropped on her knees by the chair and took Arden's cold hands in hers.

Arden opened her eyes, and smiled.

'Dear Susie!' she said.

'What is it, darling?' implored the younger girl. 'Are you ill? or—unhappy?'

Arden stooped forward, and leant her head on Susie's shoulder.

'Oh, yes,' she cried, 'I am miserably unhappy. Why didn't you—why did not some one—let me know what I was doing? I can't live, Susie; I'm sick of life—it's hateful!'

'What, Harry?' cried his sister. 'Is he bad to you—Harry?'

'Oh, no, he's good enough,' said the young bride, wearily; 'too good, I think; only I am so tired of it all—so very, very tired.'

She stopped for a little while. 'And I am only seventeen,' she went on; 'so young! How could I know what it all meant? I have been so much alone; I've never had a sister, or even a friend all of my own. How could I know, Susie, what it would be like to have some one always there, day and night, no place to call one's own? To be, soul and body, always in sight of some one else—always to be watched, looked at, talked to, kissed—oh, I have longed, longed to be alone, for just one hour, and I couldn't have it; if I said a word, he looked so grieved! And I don't want to grieve him, you know, Susie. I do love him: only it kills me to belong to him.'

'Sylvie!' cried the other girl. 'Oh, I don't know what you mean! There must be something behind.'

'And I'm so young!' moaned Arden, wearily; 'it may go on for years, and years, and years.' The tears, the young sweet-sour tears of self-pity, escaped from her closed lids and fell on to her hands.

CHAPTER XXII.

NEEDLES AND PINS.

SUSIE persuaded her mother and Harry that nothing ailed the poor little bride, beyond some natural nervousness, and an excessive fatigue. They were very kind to her, hiding their disappointment under renewed efforts to please her; and Arden tried her best to be grateful. But there was a change in her, not to be disguised. Week by week, she grew frailer and paler, and her fresh little face became quite wan and drawn. She was, however, the least presuming of daughters-in-law, never claiming any share in the ordering of the house, which she left entirely in Susie's capable hands. She quite fulfilled

Harry's promises, and sat on the sofa in her parlour all day long, reading a book over the fire. Susie took care that she should have time to herself, and without a word managed to divert Mrs. Williams from her plans of always leaving some one to keep Arden company. And so, for many hours a day, Arden might, if she chose, read or dream alone, as she had done in the old days. But in the old days the winters were not so cold and dreary, and the girl herself had not always felt so tired, so nervous, so old, so deathly sick. When the new year came round, you would not have recognised, in that pale, drawn woman, lying back, with closed eyes, the pretty girl who had looked so happy and shy at the apple-gathering. But the little household at the Farm looked at her with proud and loving eyes.

'She will be all right, now!' cried Mrs. Williams, nodding mysteriously. And

Harry's great love of her grew stronger than of old, swollen by fresh tides of tenderness and compunction.

Arden was to be a mother; that happy secret made a new gladness in every heart round the great fireside on winter evenings. But Arden herself, lying a little apart on the easiest couch, did not feel very glad. She was so ill, poor child: it seemed that there would be no end to these weary, restless nights, the sickening waking, the exhausted days. And she had a great dread of the future. Sometimes, nevertheless, she brooded tenderly over the sweet new life that should belong to her—should satisfy her, and answer all the longings of her heart; and at such times her weariness seemed a little price to pay. But they were not very frequent, these maternal impulses. Arden was not eighteen herself. It is older mothers who love their children most.

The sad, long winter dragged away, the frosty ground grew soft with February showers, the spurge-laurel broke into flower under the firs on the other side of the lane, and the deep snow melted off the pasture-lands; the cattle and the herds, long pent-up from the cold, were driven out again to grass, whisking their tails in the air, and bounding gladly, though their coats were rough and shaggy and they had lost their comfortable roundness. For since mid-December the snow had lain thick and white upon the ground, and the beasts in their dark stalls and folds had lived off dry hay and roots.

The spring was early that year, and by March the grass sprang green and fresh in the meadows, and daisies and primroses began to lift their starry heads on every bank and ridge. The buds were swelling on the bushes, though the trees were bare, or only brushed at the tops with a faint, promising red. The blackthorn was white in the hedges, the birds began to twitter, the sky cleared and lightened, fresh and blue, above the fresh greening world. The commons were a blaze of yellow gorse. Flowers springing everywhere, birds crying and calling, sunlight and sweet air, all showed the spring was here. And by the kitchen fire the weakest of the weanling lambs lay in its warm basket: every few days, Susie would bring into Arden's parlour, a flannel-covered hamper, where yellow downy chickens pecked and chirped. It was impossible to feel very miserable, in the midst of all this new, springing life: and Arden grew gay and loving as of old, taking the little lamb for walks up and down the passages, and feeding the chickens with sopped bread and beer. Perhaps it was not good for the lamb to be kept trotting about on the stone floors; and some of the fledglings certainly died from over-feeding; but no one would have dreamed of crossing Arden's fancy for them. It was so pleasant, so relieving to see her look bright and natural again.

'I've been in the house three months!' she said, one day, with a sigh. 'I should like to go out again, Harry, when you've got through with your sowing and ploughing.'

'Woo't have me drive thee to-day to Farley Common?' cried Harry, overjoyed (although last year he would not have left the 'Five Acre' to Curtis's tender mercies, for any woman alive). 'It's fair glorious upon the common, now, with the sky so blue, and the skylarks singing in it, and the gorse out in bloom, in the likeness of a sheet of gold.'

'Oh, I should like to go,' said Arden, 'if you'd care to take me!'

'That would I, my darling,' cried her husband, as he came round and kissed her. It made him so happy to serve her, when she would let him, and it was sweet to see the flush of pleasure in her pale cheeks again. Arden leant her head against his shoulder.

'I'm so glad the spring has come, Harry,' she said; 'something tells me we're going to be happy now.'

'I'm happy, Sylvie, winter and spring alike, whatever befall us, if thou'rt by my side, and out of pain.'

'Dear Harry!' said Arden, stroking one of his hands.

'Thou'rt easier, to-day, I fancy, love?'

'Oh, yes,' said Arden; 'well and contented, and in a good temper, for once.'

She laughed a quick little laugh, and with a sudden movement dragged down her husband's shock head with both her hands. 'You love your cross old wife, don't you?' she said; and looked at him with tender mockery. But she set him free without the kiss he had hoped for.

'We're quite old married people, now,' she said, as if in excuse.

'Ay, Sylvie, so it is. How can I thank you, darling, for all thou'st done for me? My happiness, my love! before I had thee I was often lonely, even with the little 'un allus after me. But now, Sylvie, there's not an empty cranny in my heart. 'Tis right full of thee, my girl; and all my days are full; so that, if I'm busy with the sowing, I think only of how thou'lt like to look at the harvest; and I look for the apple-blossom more than the fruit, 'cause you'll want to paint it, you said. And I declare if I don't think more o' the lambs than the yows, since you've taken a fancy to have them foller you about. See what a fool thou'st got for a husband, Sylvie!'

'Then you've been quite satisfied,

Harry ?' she said, with a wondering query in her voice. 'You've been happy, all these months?'

'Oh, my love, I never rightly knew what 'twas to be happy afore!'

'I'm glad,' she said; and then kept silence, wondering.

Arden went out that afternoon for her first drive. Tender hands wrapped her round and placed soft cushions at her back; but their care was all in vain. Over Farley Common the sky suddenly grew black, and the sun beat luridly upon the golden gorse. The air was still—the birds sang over-loud. Arden had alighted to pluck some primroses, and, deaf to Harry's warning, would not believe in the storm to come. She looked very pretty and wayward, with her hands full of flowers.

'But love, Sylvie,' cried Harry, 'I tell 'ee the storm's gathering overhead.'

'Look at the sun!' cried Arden; 'what

nonsense! It's only because you want to get me in.'

'Well, then, dear,' pleaded her husband, at his wits' end, 'woo't get into the cart to do me a pleasure, storm or no storm.'

'Not I!' cried Arden. 'I think it's very selfish of you to plague me so.'

'Selfish, Sylvie?' said Harry, quite bewildered.

'*Altro!* It's the first time I've enjoyed myself for months!'

'Well,' cried Harry, heroically, 'say I'm a beast—but come.'

'In a moment,' said Arden calmly, and went on gathering her posy.

Harry stood and looked at her, utterly helpless. She was going further away from the cart towards a little stream whereby some lady-smocks were lilac already. As she went, she hummed to herself an airy Italian song. She seemed in no hurry. Harry would have liked to pick her up in his arms and carry her away, but he was afraid of hurting her. She was, in fact, quite unassailable.

'Come, Sylvie, love,' said Harry in despair.

'Oh, what lovely lilies!' cried Arden, and stretched out her hands to gather the delicate white cups and rank odour of the wild garlic.

At that moment a brilliant flash of lightning ran across the common. In a minute the thunder pealed. Arden hurried to her husband. 'I'll come now, Harry,' she said, dropping her malodorous lilies, and clung to his arm like a frightened child. But it was too late. The rain fell in drenching sheets; before they reached the tethered cart they were both wet to the skin, and there was a five-mile drive before them. Before Arden reached home she was very ill, and for many days after that she lay in danger of her very life. So much was saved by skill and loving care, but when at last they carried her downstairs to lie again on the sofa in her blossom-coloured parlour, they knew that the hope of many months was dead. No child would be born with the roses to fill the wide old house with life and mirth.

CHAPTER XXIII.

OLD FRIENDS.

One warm April evening, Arden, filled with the restlessness of Spring, slid away from the busy circle by the fireside, and, seizing her gardening cloak and hat, went out into the quiet garden. She had often done so of late; for sometimes, when Harry and his sister were settling the affairs of the Farm, while Mrs. Williams dozed in her chair, a terrible sense of isolation would rush over this married child, and make her long to be indeed alone. Then she would escape into the quiet night, where the white flowers in the borders trembled dimly through the dark, and the trees were tall and dim, and the air blue above. She would pace to and fro here, calmly, till the vague yearning in her soul was soothed to rest.

But to-night there was no such dimness. The full moon lit up the furthest spaces of the clear blue sky; the stars alone were dim and flickered; all the earth lay broad and calm, washed in the pale greenish light. One could see so far, and the wide valley looked so fair that Arden did not care to linger in the garden; she loosed the watch-dog in the yard, and, wrapping her long cloak round her, she passed through the gate on to the broad white road, barred here and there with the fantastic elm-tree shadows.

How beautiful the view would be from the rise beyond the canal bridge! From there one could see in broadest day a landscape always edged with dim blue misty woods—so far could one look. And in this unearthly light the scene would indeed be strange and fair; so Arden, with Tory at her side, set bravely forth, a little wondering at her own venturesomeness, although the dangers that she ran were not appalling, for the hill was scarcely a ten minutes' walk away, and her road lay through the straggling village street.

She reached the rise, and stood to look upon the view. It was a wonderful and vague expanse, trembling in the wan light of the April morn—every detail, clear but thin, and, as it were, in profile. Fair as the valley was, the sky was fairer and more necessary to the scene; it looked as deep, and clear, and greenly blue as the still spaces of a waveless sea; and on its surface of untroubled calm, flecks of foamy cloud were splashed in airy lightness.

Arden stood and gazed, leaning against a gate. The wonderful sight took all the trouble from her soul; it was too fair to leave at once, and yet too cold to stop still. So she walked a little way further on, descending the hill on the other side, promising herself one final view from the summit, when, in a few minutes, she should turn back for home.

She herself, wandering swiftly in her dark cloak and grey dress, singing under her breath, appeared some fairy denizen of the moonlight as she flitted softly down the hill.

In the bottom, further down the lane, a young man was standing where three roads met, looking at the sign-post, almost defaced by the showers of many winters. 'To Raynham,' was clear on one of the arms, 'Clin——' was still discernible on the other, but the one which pointed ahead was past all deciphering.

'Well, it can't be Raynham, and it can't be Clin——' said Gerard Rose. 'I'll chance the other one.'

So he strode straight forwards up the rise. He walked quickly on, looking to right and left; at last he neared the top.

He stood for a moment and looked at the beautiful night.

'I presume there's an inn where I can sleep for the night. It looks a quiet, peaceful place. Dear little Arden!'

The young man, as he spoke, moved out of the shadow of the hedge in which he had been standing, and came into the light of the road. Suddenly a weak cry caught his ear, and at the same moment he perceived a shadowy outline, familiar and strange at once, standing in front of him.

'Arden!' he cried, in some alarm.

'Oh, Gerard, is it you? I was so frightened! How did you come? I thought you were in Syria.'

'Evidently not,' said Gerard; 'but, my dear child, how can they let you roam about alone at this time of night? It's very wrong.'

'They don't know I'm out,' cried Arden. 'Oh, they'll be so glad to see you! I've often talked of you.'

Gerard looked at her. 'So you're happy?' he said, with a query in his voice.

'Oh, yes. You must come home with me. You can't think what a beautiful home I've got. *Mais d'un caractère!* You'll be sketching it all day long.'

'Is that so?' said Gerard, a little surprised, for she had never seemed enraptured with the Bushes in her letters. 'But I guess I want to hear about you, Arden dear, not the house.'

'Oh, I'm all right,' said Arden; 'at least, I've been very ill. How is Mrs. Rose?'

'Ill, Arden? And they allow you—— Anyhow, it's an impossibility that you should continue here.'

'How cross you are!' said Arden. 'You might put it off until you've seen me a little longer. Oh, Gerard, it is so nice to see you again!'

'It's very "nice" to hear you say so,

every time,' said Gerard, gazing at her a little wistfully.

They were now at the bridge.

'How beautiful it is in this sweet light!' said Gerard. 'Like a forgotten page out of Shakespeare's comedies.'

'That's the house,' cried Arden; 'that black and white one, among the apple-trees. And, oh, Gerard, you mustn't be surprised if he's not quite the sort of person you expected to see. Really, you know, he's of a much older family than mine, and they've lived in that house three hundred years. And he's so good and kind.'

'A much older family than yours?' cried Gerard, in his old, gay mocking voice. 'Of course I know you're quite a special person, Arden; but, my dear girl, do tell me how one's grandfather, even yours——'

Arden began to laugh. 'Oh, you silly boy!' she cried. 'It's not grandpapa; it's Harry.'

Gerard stared at her in dumb surprise, suddenly chill and afraid.

'Didn't you get my letter?' cried Arden. 'Oh, you haven't been to Beyrout?'

Gerard shook his head.

'And you don't know?' went on Arden, rather frightened. 'Oh, Gerard, I'm married!'

For a moment the young man said nothing; he was cruelly taken aback. But the strong desire not to show Arden how deeply he was moved, helped him to keep under his anger and amazement.

'You must own it is rather a surprise!' he exclaimed.

'Yes,' said Arden. 'But come and let me show him to you. He's only a farmer, you know, Gerard.'

'Indeed!'

It was a night of surprises, certainly. Gerard felt a bitter conviction forced upon him that, however brutal the Beast might be, Beauty would find no difficulty in marrying him if there were no one else in view. But it was too bad of Arden; she must have known he cared for her.

Arden suddenly stopped.

'You're not one bit nice, Gerard!' she cried; 'you've not wished me joy or said one single kind thing. Are you ashamed of me because I've married a farmer?'

'Why no, Arden, dear,' said the young man, not without an effort. 'Only it requires more ingenuity than I possess to say kind things about a man whom I have never seen and have only heard of as "Harry," in a vague sort of way; but I'm sure he's an excellent fellow, or you would never have married him. I guess we can get along,' he added, more generously.

'Thank you, Gerard,' said Arden; 'oh, how is Miss De la Rue?'

'Miss De la Rue!' cried Gerard, amazed, 'I believe she's dying, poor girl. But how on earth did you hear of her?'

'Ellie told me,' said Arden, with a voice of profoundest sympathy.

'Told you what?' cried the other, as a dim light began to break on his mind. 'Little mischief-maker! You didn't believe her, Arden? You didn't think I could care for her? But are you going to take me in with you, Arden?'

'Of course,' she said; 'you are to stay with us. It is so nice to have a home of one's own!'

The door was open in the fearless country fashion, and, taking Gerard by the hand, she led him down the queer little passage, always breaking into flights of steps, into her blossom-coloured parlour. She left him there, and ran into the other room, where Mrs. Williams was still dozing, Susie and Harry still doing accounts, as if no great event had surprised the world since Arden left them.

'Harry,' she cried, in a quick, eager

voice, 'the most wonderful thing has happened!'

Harry looked at her. Never since he had first seen her swinging the honeysuckle trails as she walked singing down the lane, had he seen her look so gay, so young, so fair. Her eyes danced and sparkled, her lips curled up in the charming, youthful smile of a faun; she looked the very incarnation of careless love.

'Well, and whatever it be, I'm glad of it, Sylvie,' said her husband; 'you look quite your old self again, so pleasant like and well.'

'Dear old Harry!' cried Arden; 'but you'll never guess; I may as well tell you. Gerard's here!'

'Gerard!' said Harry, uneasily. He seemed to hear again the dull flap of the yellow blind against the chemist's window, to see the dim lighted room, and Arden's senseless face.

'Why, certainly,' cried Arden. 'Have

you forgotten all the times I've told you about him—my friend, who used to play with me when I was a little girl?—and you don't remember!' There were infinite reproaches in her voice.

'Yes, dearie, I remember,' cried Harry. 'I'm fair glad he's come since thou'rt so pleased to see him. Thou'st not left him in the lane?'

'No,' cried Arden, 'he's in the parlour. Oh, Harry, I am so happy and pleased!'

'And so am I, then, darling.'

'Here he is,' said Arden, as they came into the pretty white room. She went in first and Harry followed her, wearing a sheepish rustic simper of embarrassment. Gerard came forward with his handsome, nonchalant air. He stood before Arden with his fine smile, waiting for her to speak.

'Gerard,' said Arden, suddenly a little grave, 'this is my husband!'

CHAPTER XXIV.

TWO'S COMPANY.

Mrs. Williams was almost as pleased as Arden that Gerard should stay at the Farm; but she had the unusual good sense to keep to herself the plans that her motherly mind matured regarding him and Susie. 'A nice pleasant-spoken young gentleman,' she called him once to her daughter, 'far more genteel than that worthless young Masters.' But Susie's reddening cheek and flashing eye warned off this enthusiasm for comparison.

As for Gerard he troubled himself very little about the yellow-haired Susie. He felt, all the time that he acknowledged their kindness and worth, a certain irritation against these underbred, respectable, countrified people, who had deprived him of Arden in the very moment when, after much painful hesitation, he had resolved to throw prudence to the winds and marry her. He had never even dreamed that in the meantime she would marry another man; and that his successful rival should be a mere good-humoured lout of a farmer, was a galling addition to his grievance.

Nevertheless he permitted the good-humoured lout to continue his host, although a dozen times a day he reproached himself with the fact. But it was not easy to get away; for Williams pressed the new comer to remain, being anxious to please his little wife, who had recovered her old gay spirits since Gerard's arrival. Harry, for his part, was not vain, and saw no reason why his wife should not have been 'moped' in her dull quiet life with him, nor why the excitement of seeing an old friend should not dispel her melancholy. So with cordial hospitality he pressed Gerard to stay for a while. And Arden herself was so pleased, so eager, so merry; taking Gerard over all her premises, exploring barns, fowl pens, hay lofts, stables, folds, like a happy child. It would certainly be difficult to leave her, thought the young man. And, after all, no one guessed that he had come as her lover, not merely as her friend. There was no harm done to any but himself by that blunder, reasoned Gerard. He had accepted the situation, so he stayed on.

It must be owned that after the first few days Gerard's visit became a veritable trial to the slower witted farmer. Unable to retaliate, but conscious of an indefinable, unseizable antagonism at work; he was always being made to feel his own inferiority, always being reminded that he was a new comer in Arden's life. From all their reminiscences he was naturally shut out. Sometimes it flashed across him how unfit he was for the refined, graceful, delicate young girl at his side. He and Susie, she and Gerard, seemed the denizens of different spheres.

And indeed it was plain that Gerard thought the same. He did not mean to goad and torture the unhappy man, who every day felt himself sinking further and further below the level of his bride. He believed that the farmer did not understand the little half allusions with which he pointed the difference between them; but, in truth, it was Arden who did not understand; not a syllable was lost upon her husband.

Nevertheless Harry held his peace for Arden's sake, and even assented to half her praise of Gerard. Thank Heaven, it was impossible to suspect her guileless, gentle nature; she seemed more than ever sweet, more than ever undeserved, to Harry in her innocent gaiety, her childish eagerness to make her friend and her husband each admire the other. Harry would not for worlds have darkened her pretty, simple happiness.

Nevertheless it was bitter to think how recently his love had touched her. 'Do you remember?' Gerard would begin, and Arden's eyes would flash and the colour strike up her cheek; now he could never make her look so glad. Yet he was glad to see her happy; he could not (he kept saying to himself) be such a fool as to be jealous, for the dear little girl was more loving and kind to him than she had ever been before. Her nature seemed to expand in happiness, like a pimpernel in the sun. Indeed, these were very happy days to Arden, who never dreamed that Gerard could have thought of her with lover's love, nor deemed it possible that her husband could be jealous of Gerard.

One fine evening they were all sitting in the wainscoted parlour, and while Susie sang an air of Handel's, Gerard was turning her pages; Mrs. Williams stopped her talking to gaze at them with eyes of pride; and Arden and her husband, seated in the settle, talked in hushed voices not to mar the music. Susie had a fine voice, but she sang without style and dragged the time; so that to Gerard's fastidious ear her performance was a pleasure much alloyed. When he had finished thanking her and pointing out one or two *fioriture* which she might alter, Susie conscientiously sat down and tried the air again, as though he had been giving her a music lesson. Gerard, who wanted to talk to Arden, stood by her side listening with a sort of careless weariness; and while he was standing so, his eyes fell on the settle where Arden, with a bewitching pout, was lifting her arm to her husband to show a long scratch that the kitten had made. Harry stooped down and kissed the wounded wrist, saying something to his wife that made her laugh and lift her blue eyes to his face. It was a pretty, harmless little scene; but it filled Gerard with uncontrollable aversion. He longed to get Arden away, to have her to himself. Just then Susie finished.

'Bravo!' said Gerard hurriedly; 'that's much better, Miss Susie. Arden, I guess it's your turn now to come and warble.'

'Ay go, Sylvie love,' said her husband; 'thou'st forgotten thy singing of late.'

'I'm so comfortable,' said Arden lazily.

'Do come, Arden!' implored Gerard.

'It sounds so strange-like,' said the farmer, with a slow amused smile, 'to hear my wife called by her fust name. 'Tis the name of the village, you know, Mr. Rose.'

'I know,' said Gerard, 'but her old friends always called her so.'

Harry's face darkened. It was not a fortunate speech.

'I'll sing, if Harry wants me to sing,' said Arden. 'Gerard, what shall my song be to-night?'

'Sing me a song of Zion!' said the

young man. He had seated himself on the other side of her, with his arms crossed behind his head, in the corner of the settle. He looked at her.

'A hymn!' cried Susie, with round eyes.

'No, Miss Susie; I mean the other Holy City: Rome, the Eternal.'

'Shall I sing,' said Arden, 'that song the Saracen pedlars used to sing? Don't you remember when Ellie was photographed as one of those women, and I cried so because Papa wouldn't let me be done too!'

'You were nine years old then,' said Gerard.

'And you a year older. I used to think you so clever!'

'*Grazie* for the past tense! You're through with that delusion now, I presume.'

They both began to laugh, and though Arden's hand was on his arm, Harry on the further side of her began very painfully to realise that only two are company.

'Sing,' went on the young man, 'a certain song you used to know—but you must fetch your guitar!—that always seems to me the most magical thing in the world. It's Venice!' Arden shuddered, but the speaker was too engrossed with his simile to notice. He went on: 'The shady spaces of the empty vestibules we look into as we pass, and the silent women with long black shawls draping their heads and shoulders, and then beyond the cool monotony of sky and lagoon, where the quietness and lap of the waters seem another tone of the universal greyness. It's all in that song!' He began to hum it *sotto voce*.

'Oh, Gerard,' cried Arden, with tears in her voice, 'you shouldn't speak to me of Venice!'

She turned away her head and laid it on her husband's shoulder.

'Miss Susie,' said Gerard, with a despairing blandness, 'I guess I want you to sing "Despised and rejected."'

Mrs. Williams smiled through her doze.

The long evening dragged itself wearily away, but the next morning Arden came down to breakfast singing.

'It will be my birthday on Saturday,' she cried. 'I shall be eighteen!'

'Woot' like to give a party, Sylvie?' said her husband.

'There's no one to ask but grandpapa and Mrs. Lawrance. No; that would not be very gay—but I don't want to be gay.'

'Why, Sylvie, what a sigh! Thou's never growing melancholy, to be so old!' said Harry.

But Gerard was looking at her with comprehending eyes.

'I understand,' he said, in a low tone of sympathy. 'Anniversaries are cruel days. No,' he added rather louder for Harry's benefit, 'we won't keep your birthday, Arden. One doesn't feel much like exposing one's birthday at such decrepitude as that, Mr. Williams.'

The farmer chuckled slowly. 'That's a good 'un,' he said, 'that is.'

Gerard looked at Arden. 'Then that's fixed,' he said; 'we don't celebrate your birthday. Now, Mr. Williams, let us give our manly energies the task of finding out the surest way to hide that shameful fact. As for me, I don't begin to have a first idea!' but the moment after, while Harry was still chuckling over his fantastic spirits, the young fellow added—

'I have it. Let's go to Stratford-on-Avon!'

'Done,' said Harry, 'that 'ull be a good thing over. 'T'wur too wet to go theer when we wur at Leamington.'

'I know,' said Gerard quickly; he certainly did not want to revisit the scenes of their honeymoon with the bride and bridegroom.

'Oh, Gerard! how nice of you to think of it!' cried Arden. 'I've so often wanted to go!'

'I wish I'ld ha' thought of it,' said Harry meditatively; 'but what with th' yows failing, and the ploughing, and one thing and another, I've been that mazed and muddled I cud think of nothing but worries.'

And I've been so ill, too, poor old man!' said Arden.

'Ay, that's what I meant,' said Harry gratefully. 'Thou knows I doan't care much for aught else.'

'Well, I imagine I had better go upstairs and write some letters,' said Gerard, pulling out his watch. He was a little sore that when he had made the suggestion, Harry by some feminine juggle should get the credit of it. Something of this feeling inspired the note which he went to write.

'Dear Ellie,' it began—'it is now a fortnight since I encountered Arden in the lane and was borne off to her rustic home. Certainly it is very rustic, and experience teaches that while rusticity in a house is charming, the same quality as a personal adjunct is apt to pall. As a finality, I don't believe it would wear. These remarks may be taken as applying to the family Williams, who are as excellent boors as this land of beer and fog has yet turned out. It is very odd to see Arden in the midst of them; she has not yet found out their boorishness, and takes all their pretensions *au grand sérieux*. It appears to me they have a good many pretensions. The mother is a fussy old woman in a cap, who aspires to be genteel. The daughter is a serious prig, who dresses like a second-girl and aspires to Girton. As for the farmer, he has aspired so much in marrying Arden, that there is no need for him to do more than remain *le mari de Madame*. I find these people an interesting study. Their life is very narrow, very local, and they take it very much in earnest. But you must not suppose a New England earnestness. This is more material, and infinitely little concerned with the religious life. The soul, like the mind, does not exist for these prosperous country people.

'None the less there is a certain shrewdness, as distinct from ideas, under their well-nourished and dominant physique. The daughter, in particular, engages my attention. She has, I am certain, a character of no common type. There is, in her manner of turning all her fugitive and futile scraps of learning to account, a wisdom and *aplomb* one does not expect in a three-century farmhouse. Evidently she distrusts me. Sometimes, when I catch the serious gaze of her greenish, very steadfast eyes stealthily fixed upon me, I feel like shuddering. *Elle est capable de tout!* One can imagine her marching straight to her purposed end, unembarrassed by a single passion, a single pang. So much flashes out in a glance now and then; else she is a girlish, countrified, slim, and rosy creature. For her portrait, imagine Becky Sharp or Emma Bovary at sixteen. This, of course, is as she exists *in posse*; *in esse* she remains an undeveloped child. I have, however, heard of an affair with the Squire's son which for rapacious passion and cool ingenuity surpasses either prototype. Frankly, you perceive I return the compliment of her distrust.

'Arden's girlish friendship for this cold and singular *Erscheinung* has for me the fascination of that other tragic spectacle, the bird charmed by the venomous snake. Joconde herself, I believe, is not more chill, more potent, more deadly in her serpentine magic than this inexperienced Susie Williams. Life is rich in possibilities. It is these which the true artist should apprehend and immortalise. In crude reality, the possible is often disregarded. This girl, with her capabilities for infinite crime, and triumph, and influence, may doubtless marry a vulgar farmer and become a vulgar shrew. Oh, for an hour of Balzac, to seize the moment and develop it; to reveal her character in its potentiality and astonish the world with the actual realisation of the dormant evil! But Balzac is dead. Seriously, Ellie, it has occurred to me that my real sphere lies not in painting, not in a mere capture of impressions, but in the penetration of character. Sometimes I feel the divining rod twitch and jerk in my grasp.

'So much of the sister, for whom, by the way, it is clear that Mrs. Williams designs your honoured brother. There is a not unpathetic comedy in the situation. This girl, afraid of me, perceiving my grasp of her dubious past, my insight into her possibly atrocious future, doing therefore her best to conciliate me; I, interested in this problematic soul, pursuing it with ruthless penetration, plucking the heart from its mystery. Meanwhile, the old fussy, vulgar mother, sits smiling and nodding in the background, ready at any moment to weep, and smile, and cry, "Bless you, my children!"

'As for the farmer himself, he is an honest lout, a worthy boor whose soul is buried in his turnip fields, five fathom deep and more. He is evidently immensely relieved by my presence; it saves him the trouble of amusing his fine lady bride. I do not think he cares much for Arden. With that sort of man, passion is fierce but brief. Now that he is sure of her, he disregards her. Nevertheless, his narrow soul is honest, placid, incapable of resentment. He regards you with the same slow glance of amiable suspicion that his cattle lift from their pastures at the noise of your presence. Under his buffalo hide of sluggish apathy, impenetrable to the keenest darts, there exists a heart, shrivelled but kindly. I like the farmer, *per se*, but as Arden's husband I deplore him.

'As yet the revelation has not dawned. She has not yet found out that she is dying of ennui. She is still the same as ever, wonderfully "pretty-appearing," as they say at home, and with more charm than any other girl begins to have. There is a sweet incongruity in her happiness, for I fancy she is happy. I could, at times, believe her to be dead in love with him. It takes so little to satisfy a woman; give her any husband, any children, she is sure to love them; their character is a matter of detail. This, at least, is true of the Teuton woman. Perhaps it is not true of our finer and more nervous race.

'So you see, dear Ellie, there was no need of your elaborate warning. I guess I shall get along very well with the farmer, though I must allow his stamp of character is a little too much *toujours rosbif.* I believe he considers mine *toujours soufflée.* This is an obstacle to perfect mutual comprehension. But as for Arden, I am not going to make love to her. Poor child, I care for her too well to wish to hasten the day of apocalypse which surely must arrive. And I am not likely to ruin my career by a hopeless and guilty passion. After all, you know, I am from Boston, not a mere *boulevardier.*

'I am truly sorry to hear poor Nellie is so much worse. Give my best regards to her and to Colonel De la Rue. It is a pleasure to hear that the Mater is so much better in Cannes. I shall have finished my painting in a few more weeks, and then, if you feel like meeting me in Paris, we will have a good time there together before returning to the Riviera. Does that idea smile on you? If you are pleased, show your gratitude by being very lovely to poor Nellie.

'Well, good-bye, my dear El; I shall see you before long.

'Believe me, not a tragic villain,

'But your affectionate,

'GERARD.

'P.S.—You need not be alarmed at the Borgia Miss Susie; the portrait is perhaps a little " heightened " (as we said in Boston), for literary purposes. I guess we shall fix it along together.'

CHAPTER XXV.

STRATFORD-ON-AVON.

GERARD took rooms at the inn, so as to be freer for his painting; but, nevertheless, he was continually in and out of the Farm. He and Susie became excellent friends, and had many a laugh over such details of his Borgia conception of her as he chose to impart; but generally they spoke of Arden, on the rare occasions when she did not make a third in their merry banter. Gerard and Arden were indeed constantly together. He took her long drives in the spring cart, which left her rosy and fresh; and she painted at his side from the same point of view. They were such old friends, and so soon to part, that they thought the time wasted which they did not spend together ; not that Arden would have chosen to neglect her husband, but the farmer was just now overworked with the first flush of his hay harvest. He could only spare a hurried moment for breakfast and supper, dining in the hay field, so that Arden had plenty of leisure to bestow on Gerard.

The village, unused to this American liberty, formed its own opinions, and these were as scandalous as village gossip can suggest. But the household at the Farm was ignorant of these evil tongues. Mrs. Williams, Susie, Arden, and Gerard were a very merry and innocent party. And Harry, too, tried to be gay, though a sudden overmastering jealousy would sometimes choke his throat and seem to stop his heart.

But though he was jealous, Harry would not for the world have let Arden guess his misery. He did not suspect her of any one disloyal thought. He knew her to be true and good. But he remembered the pallid ailing wife whom he had striven in vain to cheer, and he looked on this gay fresh girl who enjoyed her life so well since Gerard had come. He had done her, so he would think, a grievous wrong in marrying her, who could never really love him. And then the sight of her merry face would pacify him. 'Let her be happy if she can, poor child,' he would think; and notwithstanding his secret anxiety he could not resist a hopeful mood. She was certainly happy now. Would she be happy still when Gerard had left? Such was the problem, fraught with despair and rapture, which haunted him by day and night. What would the answer be? Sometimes it seemed so clear that his wife had learned to love him at last, that Harry took the answer for spoken; and then he would be very happy. Then he would gladly upbraid himself for his jealous fancies. It was a sin to suppose the most innocent error in such a spotless life. Arden was his, only his! Let her give the overflowings and remnants of her love to whom she would.

But alas! sometimes, suddenly, unaccountably, this happy assurance would fail. He would look at his wife's pale face and reproach himself bitterly for having brought upon her a trouble that she did not comprehend; or she would sigh over some remembrance to which he had no clue; or she and Gerard would laugh at some allusion he could not guess. They were always laughing at things he could not understand! It might be they laughed at him, too!

'Are you tired, poor old man?' Arden would say, and come and lay her arms on his shoulders, stooping to look at his face. Then, at her pretty solicitude, the frown would relax; he would love her more than ever.

Arden's birthday morning dawned bright and clear. It was the 12th of June. All the wild roses were full in blow, and the streams smelt of the meadowsweet and willowherb upon their banks. The summer was early, and the dryest pastures were already cut for hay. They might have begun to mow the low-lying meadows, and in secret Harry's right arm longed to be sweeping the scythe through the flower-grown grass. But it was Arden's birthday, and her wish was doubly law.

They set out for Stratford by the morning train, four young people, Mrs. Williams having elected to stay and get their supper ready. Arden was so eager and delighted that her husband reproached himself bitterly for having so long refrained from giving her so simple a pleasure.

'Thou's been sorely moped, my love, I fear,' he said, with a sad kindness.

'Oh, no,' said Arden; 'one can't go out

in the winter, you know, Harry. But now —oh, do let us go *lots* of expeditions!'

Gerard laughed.

'Farmer Williams thinks of his standing hay!'

Now this was a little too near the truth to be quite a well-chosen pleasantry.

'I hope, young man,' said Harry grimly, 'as I think of my wife first.'

'Why, certainly,' said the incorrigible Gerard; 'don't you see I meant to make a joke?'

Arden laughed. 'We're always making jokes,' she said; and 'they're so small no one else can see them. It takes quite a long apprenticeship to see the points!'

'Ten years hence,' went on Gerard, 'we shall have you and your brother, Miss Susie, just as frivolous and inconsequential as myself; all alike corrupted by this young woman's unholy influence.'

'It seems odd,' said Susie simply, 'to think as you've known her so much; longer than we have, Mr. Rose.'

Harry said nothing, but his face grew set and cold.

Susie was the next to speak. 'Oh, look,' she cried, letting down the window, 'oh, Sylvie, Harry, there it is—there's Stratford! I was at school there, you know, Mr. Rose, when I was a little girl. Oh, Harry, promise me as you'll take me to see Miss Wakefield. 'Twould seem so strange-like not to go. And there's the river; we must row on the river.'

'That's good,' said Gerard; 'and we must go to Shakespeare's house, and see the tomb in the church, and drive to Anne Hathaway's cottage, and give ourselves dyspepsia with three-cornered Stratford cakes.'

'D'you mean Banbury cakes?' said Susie, wondering. 'I never heard ought o' Stratford cakes.'

'Oh, delightful,' cried Arden, clapping her hands; 'Gerard caught tripping! So you don't know everything at Harvard, quite? There's just a trifling point or so of local colour you can pick up better in Europe, eh, Gerard?'

Strangely enough, though this joke was very small, no one laughed at it so heartily as Farmer Williams.

The train stopped, and they got out and walked down the wide streets of the bleak little town.

'Well,' said Gerard, as he looked about him, 'I have often longed to see this place. It is the Mecca of our drama. I guess, when the "Mayflower" set out for Plymouth, the Pilgrim fathers little dreamed that of all the towns in the old country there would be none for which their children would cherish so fantastic a devotion as for the birthplace of the Stratford play-actor. Nothing strikes one so much in life as the incongruity of things. I call that an incongruity; they would have called it a degeneration; Harvard would call it the influence of culture. To me it's simply incongruous. There's a delightful humour about it. And the place itself, that's incongruous too. There's no breath of romance here; no comedy-idleness and sweetness, as there is about Guyscliff, or Stoneleigh, or Kenilworth. I can see no reason why Shakespeare should have to be born in this bare little town. It's just the one bleak, prose little place in this Elizabethan shire. All the rest is pure *paysage pour rire*, as Vernon Lee says somewhere, or Colvin, I don't know. Just the effects for a stage: low-lying meadows full of king-cups and lady-smock, the bend of a full, sleepy river, a plank bridge; or that mill at Guyscliff with the balcony for the stage Princess to come out and sing upon, and the cascade in front, with the ivied Hall breaking through the trees. And Warwick; there's an Ariosto-Fletcher magic for you! That grey enchanted castle rising mystically from the grey water overdrooped with willow-boughs! And, at the back, hilly streets of mediæval houses for the retainers to royster and fight in. There was the place for a playwright to be born! But here, as I said—I can't allow why Shakespeare should be born right here. It gives no stamp, I guess, this place!'

'Hard words break no bones,' said Harry rather grimly. 'He *wur* born here, you see, Mr. Rose.'

'I'm so sorry you don't like it!' said Susie. 'We all think it beautiful—Shakespeare's Stratford.'

'Why, certainly,' cried the young man; 'don't you see that *is* the beauty, Miss Susie? There's nothing cheap about the effect! If this town had possessed the feudal charm of Warwick, or the dreamy romance of Kenilworth, or the comedy-picturesqueness of Guyscliff, there would have been no surprise in Shakespeare having been born here. But as it is, it's touching! One thinks the man and the place intrinsically finer for their being so little in obvious relation to each other. Shakespeare is not the mere product of Stratford, nor Stratford the mere surroundings of Shakespeare. They become valuable entities! One respects the lasting attachment which the greatest poet of all time lavished on these winter-beaten streets. "It hallows him that gives and him that takes." I declare, Miss Susie, I think you are much to be envied, having lived in this town.'

'Oh,' said Susie, rather blankly; 'I'm glad you like it.'

'Isn't he clever?' cried Arden at the same moment, turning to her husband; but as she turned round she thought she caught an irreverent sentence on his lips. Surely it could not be? What?

'Fine words butter no parsnips'—so it sounded.

'Harry!' she cried; 'are you angry? Why, what's the matter?'

Perhaps if he had told her then, she would have understood in time that he felt himself neglected, but he would not cross her pleasure. He smiled to see her so eager and childish.

'Nay, nay, little maid,' he cried; 'I'm not angered. I meant it for a joke-like, as Muster Rose 'ud say.' A slow grin widened on his face at this shooting of the enemy with his own revolver.

'So glad,' said Gerard, with his fine smile; but he was rather cross. He had let all his theories be disconcerted.

They walked on in silence. 'Where shall we go first?' asked Arden.

'What difference?' said Gerard.

'Only that we must begin somewhere. I suppose a birthplace is as near a beginning as anything can be. Harry, which is the way?'

'Here we are, Sylvie!'

It was indeed the well-known, timbered house. They rang the bell and entered.

'Why, Harry,' said Arden, in a caressing whisper, 'it's not half so pretty as our house at home!'

'I've allus liked th' old house,' replied her husband in as low a voice; 'but Sylvie. love, I never thought it fit for the likes of thee!'

'I've been very happy there,' said Arden. And, as they went together through the narrow little house, all Gerard's banter failed to bring a frown to Farmer Williams' serious brow. It was a very happy party that laughed and theorised in the tumbledown brown chambers where Shakespeare played his childhood and dreamed his youth away. They liked to imagine—Arden and Gerard—the many times in which that house had seen him in disgrace; they invented superior young friends of his, who had doubtless come to see him in the back shop, and were afterwards held up as examples to him by his parents; they fancied the excuses he would make to slip away to Anne Hathaway in her pretty cottage, and discussed the attraction which an older woman has for boys of genius. Gerard had just begun upon the remonstrances of old Mr. Shakespeare when his good-for-nothing son proposed to join the strolling players, when Harry interrupted the flow of his would-be Elizabethan tongue.

'Muster Rose,' he said rather awkwardly, 'I fancy there's a fairish number o' sights we've got to see.'

'That's so,' said Gerard, comprehending in one glance the serious faces of Susie and the attendants. 'It doesn't do to mock the idol in his temple,' he whispered to Arden, as he led her out.

She laughed. Harry's face clouded over again; they were always laughing together.

They passed the old grammar school where Shakespeare got his slender schooling, and then they set out for the church, that stands so well between its broad green avenue and the sleepy river at the back. They wandered silently through the aisles, and looked at the storied tombs with their rough carving.

'Odd, isn't it?' said Gerard, 'that in the very years you always call the flowering-time of the Fine Arts in England, your grandees could get no better tombs carved for themselves than their great-great grandfathers had been accustomed to! What surface! What paucity of detail! It must have been a real martyrdom, anyway, for some travelled courtier and dabbler in Art to know that when his time came he would have to repose under the weight of such a thing as that. Shades of Pisano and Della Quercia! They all went to Italy, your lords and scholars. Why in the world did they never bring some carvers back?'

'We're in church,' interposed Susie softly; but she was quite as much shocked at the criticism as the sacrilege. It was all so fine and rare to her. Gerard bowed, and kept silence till they reached the chancel and the painted bust of Shakespeare.

'Well, I declare,' cried Gerard. 'It's the most pathetic thing I ever saw. Is this all they could do for Shakespeare?'

They stopped and looked at the portrait with interest and wonder; but, after a glance, Arden strayed away. When Gerard lowered his eyes he saw that she had moved forward, and was looking at the nearest monument.

It is indeed a contrast to the rude figure-head which stands for Shakespeare's presence in his church Two young people, in the beautiful, careless dress of the court of Charles II., are looking out of a square carved frame at the passers-by. Handsome youth and beautiful girl, undimmed by age or change, wearing their lace ruffles and bygone finery with an easy grace as out of date as these, they still look out at the altering world with a facile, indifferent interest ; as though, seated in their opera box, they were looking on at a play.

'I like them best,' said Arden, looking up. 'What a difference!' and she glanced back at the painted bust.

'Yes,' answered the young man. 'It's apocalyptic! It brings home to me, with a shock of understanding, the whole social difference between Shakespeare and his London world. The little glover's shop never told us that! But this. Oh, one understands the sonnets now! Let him be what he would, greatest tragedian since Æschylus, greatest comedy-writer of all time, friend and accepted equal of Elizabeth's finest courtiers ; one sees now that he never really was on their level. He was always hopelessly above or below them. He was Shakespeare. He was Shakespeare the glover's son. He lives for all time ; but while he lived on earth he was never the equal of these two beautiful, careless, unrenowned young people.'

'No,' said Arden. 'That's very true.'

'They had the advantage, living, certainly. Look at that vulgar painted face, with its pompous complacency of sitting for its portrait. *Bourgeois* to the end of the finger-tips! And these graceful, facile creatures, with their beautiful manners and unburdened hearts and brains. He might have created such a young fellow as that; he could not become it.'

'Yes,' said Arden again; 'I like them best.'

Harry, who for some time had been listening in growing dudgeon to Gerard's harangue, came forward at this moment. He slipped his hand almost roughly through Arden's arm, and drew her to him.

'Noan the less, my lass,' he said, 'thou's cast in thy lot with th' other side.'

CHAPTER XXVI.

LAUGHING AND CRYING.

It was hot in the hayfield; one of those days of fierce sudden heat that flit like tropic birds across the temperate changes of an English summer. The haymakers looked flushed and heated, as they wielded their pitchforks in the striking blazing sunlight. One woman, who had turned faint from the heat, was sitting in the shade on a bank; while Arden—a vision of coolness in her muslin frock and flapping Siena hat—stooped down to question her.

'You feel better now?' she inquired.

'Yes, Miss, that I do, Lor' bless you, Miss; Mum, I ought to say; as asks your pardon,' said the haymaker, rising as she spoke.

'Do you think you could walk to the house, up the shady path?'

'Lor' yes, Miss. I believe I could.'

'Then go along,' said Arden. 'You ought not to try and work again just yet. I'll set you your dinner in the cool kitchen. You'd better not try dining here with the rest. It's nearly twelve,' she added, looking at her watch.

The haymaker curtsied out her thanks, and walked away.

'*Dio! è cocente!*' cried Arden, as she threw herself down under the tree. 'But I suppose I must even face it.'

She sat for a minute or two quite still, looking at the busy scene.

'And I am dying of heat,' she mused aloud, 'sitting still in the shade in a muslin gown with a sunshade over my head. Poor things, how *can* they do it?'

'This poor thing can't do it any more!'

cried a merry voice, and Gerard, all in white linen, with a pitchfork on his shoulder, sauntered up to her, and threw himself down at her feet. "I'm killed, sire; and his chief beside, smiling the boy fell dead,"' he quoted, sighing.

'All very fine,' laughed Arden, 'but I don't think much of *your* heroic devotion. Look at Harry.'

'Look at Napoleon!' he cried. 'I never pretended to that!'

'Well, then, look at me,' said Arden.

'With all the pleasure in life! I never want to look at anything more "fine-appearing!" But I can't say I perceive the devotion—much.'

'Gerard!' she cried; 'and Harry said I had been of so much use.'

'Ornament, I should suggest,' replied the other; 'that's more in our line, I fancy, Arden. Let me see, was it three swathes of hay that you tossed over, or two. Two, I think.'

'I didn't mean that, you stupid boy! Of course I can't make hay in tight sleeves,' she exclaimed, with triumphant logic.

'Oh, no, of course not,' said Gerard humbly. 'It's so sensible to wear tight sleeves on such occasions; I might have expected it of you. Of course, you could not work!'

'All very well to laugh! I suppose you were asleep when it happened.'

'What happened?'

'Ah! I shan't say. You were asleep, evidently.'

'I did seem to perceive a piece of melodrama in the distance,' said Gerard musing, 'or perhaps I dreamed it. I appeared to notice a young woman throwing herself upon the prostrate body of a haymaker, and maliciously emptying a mysterious phial down the poor creature's eyes and mouth. She expired soon after in agonies. But I didn't seem to care to allude to the crime in your presence.'

'Gerard!' cried Arden, starting up; 'you horrid boy! Well, I'm going to get her some dinner.'

'The murdered victim?' exclaimed the young man, leaping to his feet in mock alarm. 'Not alone, misguided fair, not alone shalt thou venture into that ghastly presence.'

'Very well,' said Arden, 'come along. I don't think you're much use down here, anyway.'

'Oh, generous praise, not to be answered in words!' cried Gerard. 'My gratitude swells out my heart to silence. But if the devotion of a lifetime——'

'Open the gate!' commanded Arden, laughing. 'I shall think you have got a sunstroke next.'

They went laughing up the rutty lane, made for the carts to travel up and down by. Harry paused in his work to look after them a moment.

'Don't you want to know, Arden?'

said Gerard at last, after an interval of silence, 'don't you want to know when I am going away?'

'Going away!' Arden stopped still. 'Oh, no; I don't want to know. Don't tell me!' she cried passionately.

Gerard looked at her, surprised.

'You're overtired, dear,' he said, 'with the sun and the walk. Take my arm.'

Neither said anything, till, as they passed through the rickyard, Gerard looked at the two new golden piles.

'Before the last rick is thatched,' he said, 'I shall be gone away.'

Arden raised her eyes. 'I shall be sorry to have you go,' she said.

'And I. Very sorry. We must not lose sight of each other, Arden.'

'No,' she said. 'It's not that I'm afraid of. It's the actual saying good-bye. It kills me saying good-bye! It's like losing things by death; you feel sorry when any one dies, and wish you had done more for them. I feel like that about parting. Oh, often I have felt a kind of anguish to leave a place I have not been very specially happy in—some holiday place we have just visited and then left! I was always miserable to leave. How I used to strain my eyes to get the last look; and how I used to try and fix in my mind just the way things were arranged in the inn-parlour; because I should never see them again! I always feel that I shall never see things again. And when one's friends go, it's like wrenching a piece out of one's life.'

'Yes,' said Gerard; 'I remember, when you were a little girl, how miserable you looked when we went back to Boston. Dear little Arden, I never forgot your face then.'

'How wretched I was! I've always had that feeling about letting things go; it seems as if nothing else could ever be so precious. And do you remember Ellie's telling me to make friends of people passing through?'

'No,' said the young man. 'How like her!' He laughed softly.

'But I never did, you see,' said Arden. 'You and Ellie, my husband and his sister, are all the friends I have in the world. I have never cared very much for any one else. It will be dreadful to let you go.'

'But I shall come again, Arden, often,' he cried. 'Dear Arden, do you think that out of sight will be out of mind, with me?'

'Oh, I don't know,' she said, impatiently, 'and I don't care. What have I to do with the future? I don't understand it; I can't feel that it's real: it's all blank, dim—ghosts without faces.'

She covered her eyes with her hand, and leaned her arms upon the high gate that led into the yard. After a moment she looked up.

'No, I can dream back the past, but I can't realise meeting again, not even papa.'

'Come in, Arden,' cried the young man,

drawing her by the hand. 'You must come in; you'll be ill.'

They went in to the pretty blossom-coloured parlour, cool and fresh after the heat. 'I can't sit down yet,' said Arden, 'I must go and get the woman her dinner.' She went out, and Gerard, left alone, took down from the wall her well-remembered guitar, and began to thrum on it idly, as he recalled Italy, his childhood, Arden. As he was playing she slipped in behind him, and stood listening in the doorway, till he began to sing, still very softly, some quaint pifferari song, 'Bella Roma—mai lasciar.'

Arden glided forward quietly and suddenly.

'Oh, give it me back,' she cried—'my old life; I was so happy then, so happy. Why did it not last? But it's gone, and it can never come over again—never—never.'

She sank into a chair, crying bitterly.

CHAPTER XXVII.

THE WITNESSES.

Harry stayed in the hay meadow, working harder than his labourers. He only stopped one moment, to glance at Arden as she flitted out of the field in her fresh white dress, and then he gave a proud sigh. "'Twasn't for naught, as I told the old gen'leman, Sylvie 'ud never break her back o'er the work,' he chuckled to himself as he set to making hay with redoubled energy. It inspired him, in the hot blazing field, with the seed of the hay pricking his eyes, while his back ached and his hard hands blistered with the strenuous tossing and lifting; it inspirited him and refreshed him to recall that gay sweet vision, white and cool, whom his labour kept so far from toil. Only the brightest thoughts visited the farmer this morning, for looking on the abundant harvest of the field, with over the hedge the full-eared corn already turning pale yellow, it was impossible to fancy anything but prosperity in store.

But perhaps his previous anxieties had told upon him, perhaps his energy was too violent, for after a few minutes Harry staggered and nearly fell. He recovered his balance and stood leaning on his pitchfork, while the air swam with lights before his eyes and surged into his ears, something seemed to snap in his brain, and every moment the sense of being drawn back into nothingness would recur, but less forcibly time by time. At last the farmer was able to stand erect; he tossed the pitchfork away.

'Neil,' he called, 'I've got a bit of a stroke, I fear. 'Tis naught, man, naught to be afeard on. I'll just step up to th' 'ouse and stop work a bit. You'll look arter the men.'

He walked out of the field, half sorry to have to leave his labourers, and half pleased to think of Arden's nursing. How good she had been to poor Maggie Jones! It was almost worth while being ill in the midst of the harvesting, to come in for her tender kindness, to feel her soft hands cooling his brow, to hear her anxious, fearful voice; at least so Harry fancied.

He reached the house, and went straight up to their bedroom, that he might wash and brush away, as much as might be, the traces of his illness before showing himself to Arden. It was characteristic of the man, that even when he longed for her sympathy most, he tried to disguise his illness lest it should frighten her. The face he saw in the glass looked so purpled and heavy that it took himself aback.

'It's well,' he muttered, 'as I didn't go

straight in. I should ha' frightened the poor little maid out o' her seven senses.'

There was still a great noise rushing in his ears, so that all sound was uncertain; but Harry thought he recognised the thin notes of the guitar. He imagined Arden sitting alone in the little parlour (for in his confused illness he had forgotten Gerard), sitting alone and suddenly seeing him ill, letting go her instrument and running to wait upon him. The impulse of tenderness that this image awoke was so strong in Harry's heart that he felt he must see her at once. He could not wait to put himself in order; he would just look from the door that opened on the little stair leading down; he would only look through the door and glance at her, and retreat before she could see him. His hand was on the knob, and as the door opened the music floated in. Yes, it was the guitar, suddenly, unaccountably it stopped; and then crying! Was that a woman's crying? In his eagerness

Harry stepped out on to the staircase. There beneath him, on the low chair by the hearth, the chair they had chosen together at Warwick, Sylvie was crouched, sobbing desperately. Gerard was kneeling at her side; he had caught one of her hands; he was begging her to stop, but she went on crying.

'I was so happy, so happy then; and it can never come back.'

It was a terrible reaction from his dreams. He felt the blood rushing to his head, and a blind fury coming over him from without, like a cloud. A desire to strike, kill, destroy, that was not anger. For he was, in his inner self, sensible of no violent wrath, only of a terrible despair. She did not love him, then. He had not been able to make her happy. He had ruined her life, hopelessly, beyond restitution. She was crying, and he could not console her. That youth down there might have consoled her; they loved each other.

All this he dimly felt, while the blood surged and thundered through his veins; while he saw everything turn red, and bright lights beat in his eyes, while a new fierce, strange desire to leap out and murder, awoke in him like an appetite, like the sudden instinct of the tiger tasting blood.

At last he cried out, and Arden lifted her face. How pale she was!

The sight of her awoke the impulse to shield her, which had dominated him so long that it was dominant still, unconsciously, even in this chaos of passion and loss. She must not be frightened, she must not be frightened! The thought came to him as a natural habit, and it saved him from murder.

He came downstairs heavily, slowly, passing by Gerard and taking Arden's hand. She clung to his shoulder with the other arm, crying out that something had happened.

'Ay, ay,' he said, 'summat's happened. Summat as has happened often afore, and 'ull often happen agen; but it shan't hurt thee. Sylvie, more nor I can help. What was I saying?'

Again the sense of failing and darkness took him; he groped for a moment with his hand. It touched Gerard, standing irresolute on the hearth. Harry drew it back, with a swift impulse of loathing.

'You'ld better go, young man,' he said; 'it's best you keep away. I doan't bear 'ee no ill-will, but I can't rightly stomach the sight of 'ee. Sylvie, is there any one in th' 'ouse?'

She told him, sobbing with vague fear, that his mother and the servants were in the kitchen, drawing the beer for the men; and the sick harvester was there also.

'Ay, ay; call 'em all in,' he said, 'all on 'em as you can find. It's all I can do for you, little 'un; all I can do. It 'ull show 'em all as I trusted you. But doan't 'ee cry, Sylvie; thou's a young woman, thy life's all to come. Well, well! Tell 'em I'm in the brown parlour. I'll be there as soon as any. It's all I can do,' he muttered to himself, as he staggered heavily across the passage. 'Poor little maid, I can't set her free and I can't make her love me. I can but trusten her.'

He stooped down when he had reached the other room, looking for something in the old bureau where he kept his ledgers, and when he raised himself with the parchment in his hand he saw Sylvie, his stepmother, and three or four of the Farm servants huddled together in the doorway. Mrs. Williams sprang forward, but he put her aside with a gentle authority not to be denied. His face looked very grey, and his voice was weak and thick. The group in the doorway looked at him for orders: they had a confused notion that he meant to stop the harvest.

'Sit ye down,' said Harry at last, 'sit

ye down over there and listen. I'm a going to read you my will. Curtis, Kingston, Swinburne, here, you witness as I sign my name—and now listen, all on you—Mrs. Jones and all—ay Neil, there you are. You're the witnesses.'

He stopped a moment; no one dared to speak, but Arden gave him one swift appealing glance. She could not understand what it all meant, it was all a dreadful, clueless mystery. 'Nay, Sylvie,' he said, 'doan't 'ee cross me. I'm that moithered I can't rightly think. . . . I got it done the day th' insurance officer refused me. Well, I'm glad on it now, glad on it now . . . .'

His voice died away, and he remained for a moment silent, his face vague and almost meaningless, a dazed look in his bloodshot eyes; but the silence remained unbroken. Arden had fainted unnoticed.

'Yes,' he went on, speaking as if to himself, 'I got it done when we wur in Leamington together. And th' insurance officer refused my life—a bald, fattish man with a blear eye, he wur. I niver liked the looks of him. But I thought: "Well, old chap, say what you like, it shan't make any difference to her; she shan't be any the wuss for it, I can tell you, the poor little maid."'

A smile played over his lips. He seemed to forget his hearers.

'And yet,' he went on, 'I never thought o' proving it. I might ha' dropped down sudden and left her with her thirds, as if I'd no call to make it good to her. But it's all signed fair and clear, all fair and clear, afore the witnesses.'

The words seemed to rouse him from his retrospect.

'You're the witnesses, remember,' thundered Harry, 'and, as you look for the kingdom of Heaven, I charge you all that you allus say and swear that this is my true will and testament. And if so be's the Devil and the powers of them below should ever lead me away to sign aught different it's to be o' no account, them other wills. Doan't you think it binding, if ever I be so led away as to say aught agen a second marriage. I *might* go mad. I feel it,' said Harry softly; 'there's such a spinning and roiling in my head as though I were Raynham mill-wheel churning the water, turning and turning for ever.' He put up his hand to his head for a moment, with the pathetic wonder of a strong man suddenly ill. 'But I'm sound enough now,' he went on— 'sane in mind and body, as the dockment runs.'

Mrs. Williams had started to her feet at the mention of the pain in Harry's head. She only waited for his voice to stop to break out into wailing lamentations.

'Oh, th' arrow leaves!' she began, 'where's Susie put the powdered yarrow leaves? I allus keep 'em all ground up and handy, these ten years and more ; and now, now, she's got the key down in the hayfield.'

'Nay, mother,' said Harry, 'sit ye down. There 'll be time enough for talking and doctoring arter.'

He took the opened parchment in his hand and rose to his feet, as if in reverence of the occasion. The servants rose too, and Mrs. Williams, who was sobbing loudly with her handkerchief pressed to her eyes ; but Arden, scarcely recovered from her faint, lay back unmoved and almost insensible. It did not seem to touch her, this strange and fearful scene, or to be more real than the memory of dreams that haunt us on the brink of waking. She lay back wearily, as if suffering it to have its way.

'This is my last will and testament,' began the farmer, in a sing-song drawling voice, quite unlike his passionate utterance, 'written this second day o' December,

I being then sound and sane o' mind and body, in the Bath Hotel at Leamington.

'Whereby I leave to my dear and much-loved sister, Susan Williams, the cottage in Wood Lane with the garden appertaining, and the three cottages known as Ford End with all lands and appertanences thereto; and these I leave her with my love.

'And I leave my stepmother, Sarianna Williams, th' interest of five hundred pounds Consols for the term of her natural life, the same being half of the fortune left me by my mother Margaret Williams, in her own right, which I bequeath now to her that has been a second mother to me, the same to go at decease of th' aforesaid Sarianna Williams to th' aforesaid Susan. And I bequeath the aforesaid Sarianna the cottages at th' end of th' orchard, for the term of her natural life, to descend thereafter to the aforesaid Susan.'

'Oh, Harry!' sobbed Mrs. Williams, but she dared say no more.

'And all the rest of my land, property, furniture, and estate in whativer kind, the two hunderd acre o' land with the 'ouse and buildings appertaining known as Williams' Farm, the land and 'ouse in Preston parish known as th' Apple Tree Farm, the five hundred pound Consols being the other moiety of my mother's private fortin and the seven hundred pound in Warwick Bank I leave, in testimony of the perfect trust and love I bear her, to the absolute disposal and control of my dearly beloved and honoured wife—my dearly beloved wife—Sylvie!'

The husky sing-song tones were suddenly broken through by a choking cry.

'Sylvie!' he called again; but, as she rose, he did not look at her or seem to see her, staring round wildly with bloodshot, eyes.

'It's come,' he cried at last. 'Thou's

free, Sylvie.' He fell heavily to one side, like a tree cut through at a stroke, his head striking against the corner of the settle with a heavy sound. He did not move; he did not even groan, but lay just as he had fallen on the floor.

Arden sprang forward, dazed, aghast. She flung herself down upon the floor, peering into the dead man's face, kissing his hands, calling on him wildly.

'Harry, Harry,' she kept on crying and calling, 'look at me, speak to me only, dear Harry! I can't live without you. Oh, my husband, my love; I can't let you go, Harry! Oh, God! he doesn't understand!'

Alas! No. It was too late; he would never understand. The one word that might have saved him could never reach his palsied brain. He had died for the want of it, and now he could not hear.

But all through the afternoon and through the night, long after the doctor had pronounced the last fluttering, impotent breath of life extinct, Arden sat upstairs, dry-eyed, in a still chamber, with her dead husband's head lying in her lap. She did not weep; but every now and then the air was rent with a sighing, gasping cry; and every now and then those who passed outside the closed door would hear her calling frantically on the deaf, unconscious man, who had never denied her slightest wish before, who would not hear her now, though she broke her heart with calling.

And side by side downstairs two other women crouched, weeping bitterly, and shuddering afresh at every echo of her cries.

CHAPTER XXVIII.

AFTERWARDS.

The harvest was all gathered in, the harvest that no master surveyed with pride. The house was quiet and desolate, there would be that year no merry-making. The master was dead and in his grave. Two women, clad in crape and very pale, occupied the blossom-coloured bridal parlour.

'And you will not stay and help me?' Arden was saying. She looked ill, but there was no fear now that she would lose her reason or her life. Horror, not grief, had threatened to turn her brain, and the horror was past. She had grown familiar with the cold, holy look on Harry's face. It only spoke to her now of love and loss.

'I can't, Sylvie,' said her stepmother-in-law. 'I'm sorry for you enough, poor child, goodness knows. I wish I could have been of more assistance. But there's Susie to think of first.'

'Yes,' said Arden. He was dead who had given his first thoughts to her.

'Dr. Grant's quite positive,' went on Mrs. Williams, 'as she'll recover if I take her away at once. He says he knows a lady at Warwick who was quite as wasted, and she recovered. She must stay at least a year, he says, and we're to travel about as much as may be, so as to keep her mind off it. I don't know how we could have afforded it, but for you, Sylvie.'

'Poor Susie,' sighed the widow, 'poor, poor Susie!'

'I wish she'd consent to see you, Sylvie,' went on the other. ''Tisn't my fault; but, poor child, she is not answerable for her actions. She keeps crying out against you; it's terrible to sit by and listen.'

Arden shuddered.

'There, there,' cried Mrs. Williams, 'you mustn't take it so to heart. She don't know what she's saying, poor child. But you mustn't fret if I can't make her see you, Sylvie. I daren't so much as speak of you before her, even to tell her of the deed of gift.'

'There is no need,' said Arden, in the same colourless, unvarying voice. 'I would rather you did not tell her now. When she gets well you shall tell her, and she will be glad to come back to the old place. I shall be gone then.'

'And what will you do with yourself, Sylvie?' asked the little old woman, kindly.

'I shall go back to Rome,' said Arden; 'I would like to do some good with Harry's money, but I don't know how. I shall paint, I think: I shall find something to do.'

'Yes,' said Mrs. Williams. 'But I meant about the property.'

'The lawyer tells me the tenants are all right. There's nothing here for me to see after It's for you, now, to see after a tenant for the farm. It's Susie's now. As for me, I had better go home; I don't understand this country.'

'Ah, poor child,' said the other; 'you'd best get back to your own ways and your own friends. You're not fit to rough it among the likes of farmers and such like.'

'No,' said Arden, quietly. 'I don't think I am fit to live.'

'Poor child, poor child!' repeated the older woman tenderly, smoothing the little hand that lay on the window ledge. 'I'm sure I wish I was free to give my mind to nursing you up.'

'You have been very kind,' said Arden, and she bent down and kissed the wrinkled prettiness of Mrs. Williams' face. 'I think you saved my life; and you might have hated me, like Susie.'

'La, Sylvie!' cried the older woman; but Arden had gone, had drifted away from her side.

It was now a month since the farmer had fallen down dead, so suddenly, never to move again. Susie had nearly died of grief: of silent, overmastering grief; and now there was but a hope of life. She was young, she might recover, but the shock of her brother's death had terribly shaken her in mind and body. Her love for Harry was as old as her life, it had been the very mainspring of her life; and now he was dead. As the conviction of his jealousy forced itself upon her mind she had grown to hate the frail slight nature which had, unwittingly, goaded him to death. She could not bear to hear any one speak of Arden. The poor young widow would have been terribly desolate but for kind little Mrs. Williams, who, forced for the first time in her life to take the lead in an emergency, surprised no one more than herself by her skill and courage. Everything had been left to her; all the arrangements. So that when Arden left her she had no time to sit and muse on cruel destiny, like the young widow upstairs. She went to finish the necessary packing.

They were to start for Normandy next day, she and Susie. The one hope of saving the girl lay in change; they were to start as soon as possible, and there was much to be done first. Not the least difficult of the tasks which the little old lady had set herself, was the persuading Susie to say good-bye to her sister-in law.

It was long before she succeeded. But at last, in the morning, when their boxes were being heaped upon the waggon, Susie gave in. Mrs. Williams ran to summon Arden, who was haunting the corridor like a lonely ghost. 'Come in, Sylvie,' she cried, with a gleam of brightness in her tear-swollen eyes. Arden entered.

Susie was seated on the foot of the bed, dressed all ready for her journey. There was a terrible alteration in her face, her features looked large and stern, now that the flesh had fallen away from her cheeks, and her blue eyes were hollow and large, with an implacable glitter in them.

'Susie!' cried the other girl, falling on her knees by her side.

'Get up,' said Susie, sternly.

Arden obeyed. She stood looking at her sister-in-law; she forgot to think of herself, she was so sorry for her.

'Can you forgive me, Susie?' she said at last.

Susie did not answer.

'Oh, Susie, Susie!' cried Arden, terrified at a resentment incomprehensible to her. 'You can't go away like this and leave me. We may never see each other again; and I, too, am miserable. I've lost him, too. Look at me kindly once, Susie, for good-bye; you're *his* sister.'

'Yes,' said Susie; 'good-bye.'

She held out her hand, but not willingly; rather as if she would accomplish a promised hateful task. Arden seized the little hand and stood holding it.

'Why won't you look at me, Susie?' she said. 'It was not my fault, God knows.'

'It was not your fault, I suppose!' said Susie, looking at the weeping girl with severe unpardoning eyes; 'it was not your fault, but it was your nature; and I shall never forgive you.'

Arden looked at her a moment, but she saw it was hopeless to plead. Besides, she thought Susie under a delusion, and dared not cross her deranged fancy. 'Good-bye, my dear little sister,' she said, very sadly, and loosed her clasp. Then she turned away, and left the girl alone with her mother.

Arden had no mother to console her. She went into her little white parlour, bare now, and stripped of her treasures, for the new tenant was coming in within a week. She sat by the window and looked drearily out, while Curtis and Neil placed the old-fashioned luggage on the waggon. Then the trap came round, and Susie, closely veiled, got in. Mrs. Williams ran into the parlour, and kissed Arden. 'Good-bye, my other daughter!' she cried; then she, too, got into the spring-cart, and they drove away, leaving Arden alone behind. She sat there till dinner-time, when she could not eat; but afterwards she went upstairs, and began, wearily enough, to drag out her boxes and fold her clothes.

It was growing dusk when she heard a voice in the hall; it was Mrs. Lawrance's voice. She ran down, glad of the familiar sound.

'Come in, come in,' she cried ; 'I am so glad you are come!'

'Oh, Sylvie!' cried the elder woman, 'I'm sure I've intended coming every minute, but your grandpa's that ill I couldn't bring my mind to leave 'im ; and this marning, when I heard as they'd left you alone, I sent over for Mrs. Willis to come and keep 'im company, so's I might come round and see you.'

'Thank you,' said Arden, sitting down on the red-covered bench by her visitor's side. 'It was good and kind of you to come. I'm sorry grandpapa is ill.'

'Oh, Sylvie,' said Mrs. Lawrance, beginning to cry, 'most likely 'tis sent as a judgment upon me, as couldn't endure to be out of his thärts, so jealous and exacting as I was! Oh, the judgments of God are terrible hard to bear! I foller him about day and night, up and down the stairs, traipsing in and out of all the rooms; I never dare to leave him a moment; and yet he don't appear to reckernise me.'

'Who?' said Arden. 'What is it? What new trouble?'

'You may well say that,' sobbed Mrs. Lawrance. 'Oh, I mind me so well how he was accustomed to say they never came single. So clever and infarmed as he allus was. And now, now——'

'Tell me,' said Arden, softly; 'don't cry; let me help you, if I can.'

'You're a good child,' said the elder woman, gratefully. 'But I don't rightly know how to explain it, Sylvie. He's been terrible shakey all this 'ear; I've often told yer so. And the shock o' Williams' misfortin was too much for him. We're both in the same boat, Sylvie, you and I.'

'What,' cried Arden, 'is he dead?'

'Not in his corporal state; but his mind's dead, Sylvie, his mind's dead. He as allus was so clever, too! He's forgotten me, and aäl the time we've lived together. He rambles aäl over the 'ouse, looking for your father, child. Door after door, he opens them, and "John!" he calls; and then, when the room's empty, as it allus is, he turns round to me, and says, "Mrs. Warner," he says, as you know was my name afore he married me, "I think my son must have gone out."'

'It's dreadful!' said Arden, horror-struck.

'So it is, child, so it is. And aäl day long, it's the self-same weary search, over and over again, in aäl the rooms, and it's allus John, he wants, or his first wife. And if I make so bold as to touch his sleeve, and say, "Won't you sit down a bit, dear?" he turns quite sharply round, and speaks to me as if I was a stranger.'

'I am sorry from my heart,' cried Arden. 'Poor Mrs. Lawrance!'

'Yes, Sylvie,' went on the elder

woman. 'I've aften and aften felt repentant as I didn't love you better; but I was so swallowed up in your grandpa'; I never thaät of anything but 'im. And now I'm gone clean out of his mind. I'm no more use to him than any other woman—only to keep him out o' the way o' the furniture, and see as he don't stumble on the stairs.'

She could not speak for a minute; then she went on again in a weak, broken voice—

'At last, I'm put to it so, I've come to ask your assistance, Sylvie. I'm fair exhausted, traipsing early and late; and it flashed across me, as, may be, you'd come and help nurse; you being homeless-like yourself, with your husband dead; and in trouble, so jealous as he was.'

'Jealous!' cried Arden, starting to her feet, her eyes flashing. 'Do they say that—jealous? But they don't know,' she went on, in a softer tone; 'no one can know, but I, how good, and generous, and noble he was, my Harry!' She stood for a moment, her hands clasped, looking before her with shining eyes. Then she came up to the elder woman, who was still sitting on the ottoman, and still crying. 'Come, Mrs. Lawrance,' she said, 'take me home with you. Let us try together if we cannot help poor grandpapa.'

EPILOGUE.

It was a warm spring morning at the Bushes. Mrs. Lawrance was standing in the porch speaking earnestly to Gerard Rose.

'I'm none so disconcerted as she was out, Mr. Rose,' she was saying, 'since it's affarded me th' opportunity of putting in a word. I'm sure you've my best wishes, if they'll do you any good. T'was allus my opinion as you'd have made her a better 'usband than that poor hot-tempered Harry Williams, as she worships like a saint.'

'Does she?' said Gerard eagerly, a little surprised.

'La, yes. She never seems to so much

as think of anything without a reference to what e'ld ha' thaüt of it. But, as I was saying, you're much more fitted for Sylvie than the likes of he—though it 'ull be bitter to spare the child—she's the sunshine of the place, I allus say.'

'She was always so sweet and gay,' said Gerard.

'*I* remember when she was very different,' said Mrs. Lawrance; 'but now she's so considerate and has such a way with her as her poor granpa 'ull do anything for her, though he allus calls her by her mother's name.'

'Indeed; and where shall I find her?' asked Gerard.

'Most likely she'll be coming over the fields from the churchyard. She's been to lay some vi'lets on Williams' grave. She'll be coming back by now, for dinner's at 'alf-past one,' said Mrs. Lawrance, pulling out her watch.

Gerard took his leave and walked towards the fields. He had got as far as the canal bridge, where he had stood with Arden two years ago, where he had first heard of her marriage, when he saw her in front of him coming down the hill. She did not see him, for her eyes were looking far away beyond the horizon; a very sweet and patient gentleness was in her face and bearing. When she came near the bridge, she saw him standing near her.

'Gerard!' she said, without any surprise.

'Yes, Arden, I came to see you. I want to know if you are well and happy.'

'Oh, yes!' said Arden softly, 'I am waiting in peace.'

Gerard looked at her with a certain exasperation. He would rather she had been less calm, less contented. Still he felt awed by her aloofness.

'I am happy now,' she went on, 'for I have been sitting by Harry's grave. I always feel so quiet there, so sure of meeting him again. It is just such a day to-day as it was the spring before last, when he took me to Farley. Ah, you were not there.'

'No,' said Gerard; 'but are you going to live here, Arden, in this village?'

'I don't know,' she said. 'Grandpapa wants me now. I am able to be of some use. And soon my sister and her mother will be coming home. Susie wrote to me yesterday.'

'Don't you ever look back?' cried Gerard, a little impatiently; 'don't you regret the old life? Don't you wish ever to come back to Italy—to Rome?'

'Yes,' said Arden, 'I look back. I think how much happier I ought to have been. I think how discontented I was with my happiness. And I try and learn to be content and patient, and to care for other people, like Harry.'

The tears had risen to her eyes; she looked dreamily away.

'You never understood him, Gerard,' she said. 'No. I don't want to go back to Italy, I think; not for always. I should feel so far away from him there; he never went there. But this was his home; he always lived here. And the places he has left me belonged to him, and I can do all the things for him that he meant to have done; and the people all knew him. They lived on his land and took his wage, and I belong to him too, more here than anywhere else. He never seems very far off from me—Harry!'

Gerald looked at her for a moment. Yes, there was something unreal in the sweet passion that lit up her face. Yet none the less she looked happy; and stronger, too, than she had seemed two years ago. Then he held out his hand.

'Good-bye, dear,' he said; 'I cannot stay any longer now.'

'Good-bye,' said Arden. She did not ask him to stay.

Something fell out of her dress as she moved her arm. Gerard stooped and picked it up for her. It was a little bunch of the violets she had laid upon her husband's grave.

THE END.

www.ingramcontent.com/pod-product-compliance
Lightning Source LLC
Chambersburg PA
CBHW020805230426
43666CB00007B/870